MW01284324

Spain Travel Guide: Activities, Food, Drinks, Barcelona, Madrid, Valencia, Seville, Zaragoza, Malaga, Murcia, Palma de Mallorca, Las Palmas de Gran Canaria, Bilbao, Alicante, Cordoba, Granada, San Sebastian, Navarran Pyrenees, Costa Brava

Table of Contents

3

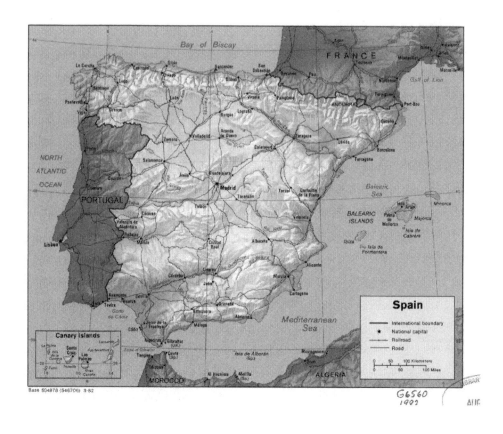

Spain

— International boundary
★ National capital
┈┈ Railroad
— Road

Base 504878 (546706) 3-82

G6560
1982
AUS

Introduction

www.Chrystal-Clear.com

Passionate, sophisticated and devoted to living the good life, Spain is both a stereotype come to life and a country more diverse than you ever imagined.

An Epic Land

Spain's diverse landscapes stir the soul. The Pyrenees and the Picos de Europa are as beautiful as any mountain range on the continent, while the snowcapped Sierra Nevada rises up improbably from the sun-baked plains of Andalucía; these are hiking destinations of the highest order. The wildly beautiful cliffs of Spain's Atlantic northwest are offset by the charming coves of the Mediterranean. And everywhere you go, villages of timeless beauty perch on hilltops, huddle in valleys and cling to coastal outcrops as tiny but resilient outposts of Old Spain.

A Culinary Feast

Food and wine are national obsessions in Spain, and with good reason. The touchstones of Spanish cooking are deceptively simple: incalculable variety, traditional recipes handed down through the generations, and an innate willingness to experiment and see what comes out of the kitchen laboratory. You may experience the best meal ever via tapas in an earthy bar where everyone's shouting, or via a meal prepared by a celebrity chef in the refined surrounds of a Michelin-starred restaurant. Either way, the breadth of gastronomic experience that awaits you is breathtaking.

Art Imitates Life

Poignantly windswept Roman ruins, cathedrals of rare power and incomparable jewels of Islamic architecture speak of a country where the great civilisations of history have risen, fallen and left behind their indelible mark. More recently, what other country could produce such rebellious and relentlessly creative spirits as Salvador Dalí, Pablo Picasso and Antoni Gaudí and place them front and centre in public life? Here, grand monuments to the past coexist alongside architectural creations of such daring that it becomes clear Spain's future will be every bit as original as its past.

Fiestas & Flamenco

For all the talk of Spain's history, this is a country that lives very much in the present and there's a reason 'fiesta' is one of the best-known words in the Spanish language – life itself is a fiesta here and everyone seems to be invited. Perhaps you'll sense it along a crowded, postmidnight street when all the world has come out to play. Or maybe that moment will come when a flamenco performer touches something deep in your soul. Whenever it happens, you'll find yourself nodding in recognition: this is Spain.

Land of the siesta, daily life in Spain moves slowly and runs late. Many travelers can get frustrated by the limited store hours and seemingly laid back pace of life. But it's this Spanish perspective — move slowly, enjoy yourself, eat well, and relax — which gives the country so much character – and why I keep coming back, over and over again. Spain is a beautiful, interesting, and dynamic country with a lot of regional uniqueness and variety. Madrid and Barcelona are hip and energetic cities, Granada has a Moorish touch, Basque Country up north contrast itself to Southern living. The Spaniards love visitors, hosting strangers, drinking good wine, laughing at a good meal, and enjoying life. A fiery, passionate place, this country will stay withy you forever and, unlike other Western European countries, will be a lot kinder to your wallet.

If you're visiting Spain for the first time, be warned: this is a country that fast becomes an addiction. You might intend to come just for a beach holiday, a walking tour or a city break, but before you know it you'll find yourself hooked by something quite different – the wild celebration of some local fiesta, perhaps, or the otherworldly architecture of Barcelona. Even in the best-known places to visit – from the capital, Madrid, to the costas, from the high Pyrenees to the Moorish cities of the south – there are genuinely surprising attractions at every turn, whether it's hip restaurants in the Basque country, the wild landscapes of the central plains, or cutting-edge galleries in the industrial north. Soon, you'll notice that there is not just one Spain but many – and indeed, Spaniards themselves often speak of Las Españas (the Spains).

Partly, this is down to an almost obsessive regionalism, stemming from the creation in the late 1970s of seventeen comunidades autonomías – autonomous regions – with their own governments, budgets and cultural ministries, even police forces. You might think you are on holiday in Spain – your hosts may be adamant that you're actually visiting

Catalunya, and will point to a whole range of differences in language, culture and artistic traditions, not to mention social attitudes and politics. Indeed, the old days of a unified nation, governed with a firm hand from Madrid, seem to have gone forever, as the separate kingdoms that made up the original Spanish state reassert themselves in an essentially federal structure.

Does any of this matter for visitors? As a rule – not really, since few tourists have the time or inclination to immerse themselves in contemporary Spanish political discourse. Far more important is to look beyond the clichés of paella, matadors, sangría and siesta if you're to get the best out of a visit to this amazingly diverse country.

Even in the most over-touristed resorts of the Costa del Sol, you'll be able to find an authentic bar or restaurant where the locals eat, and a village not far away where an age-old bullfighting tradition owes nothing to tourism. The large cities of the north, from Barcelona to Bilbao, have reinvented themselves as essential cultural destinations (and they don't all close down for hours for a kip every afternoon). And when the world now looks to Spain for culinary inspiration – the country has some of the most acclaimed chefs and innovative restaurants in the world – it's clear that things have changed. Spain, despite the current economic uncertainty, sees itself very differently from a generation ago. So should you – prepare to be surprised.

Typical Costs

Accommodation – Accommodation in Spain is pretty cheap when compared to other Western European countries. Dorm beds in hostels typically begin around 15 EUR per night and go as high as 30 EUR in major cities like Barcelona or Madrid. Hostel private rooms start around 40 EUR per night for a double. Free WiFi is standard, and it's not uncommon to find hostels with free breakfast, either. Budget hotels begin around 45 EUR for a twin/double and go up from there. Prices will be slightly lower outside of the major cities and tourist areas. Airbnb is common in most major cities, with shared accommodation starting around 25 EUR per night. For a private home or apartment, expect to pay at least 80 EUR per night. There are also over 400 campsites across Spain offering basic facilities to those who travel with a tent. Campground Prices start around 15 EUR per night.

Food – You can get cheap tapas and sandwiches meals for between 3-7 EUR. If you want wine included, expect to spend about 10-13 EUR per meal. A good restaurant meal will set you back around 13 EUR. If you go out for paella, drinks, or appetizers, then you should plan to spend around 22 EUR for a meal. Spain has a lot of expensive restaurants, and meals there begin around 27 EUR with a drink. Fast food like McDonalds and Maoz cost around 7 EUR. Groceries will cost around 25-30 EUR per week, especially if you stick to the copious local markets around the country. You'll find the cheapest (and freshest!) produce and meat at the local markets.

Transportation – City metro and bus lines cost 1-3 EUR per trip. The train system (Renfe) can be expensive. High-speed trains can cost between 50-140 EUR, depending on distance and how popular the route is. Slower regional trains range between 15-45 EUR per trip. Overnight buses are the cheapest inter-city option and cost around 18 EUR. When it comes to flying, your cheapest options will likely come from Madrid or Barcelona. Both cities offer flights to most hubs around the world, making them the most convenient and budget-friendly choices for flight arrivals and departures.

Activities – Museums and attractions in Spain cost between 2-14 EUR. Diving on the islands will cost around 45 EUR per dive.

Suggested daily budget – 50-60 EUR / 52-62 USD (Note: This is a suggested budget assuming you're staying in a hostel, eating out a little, cooking most of your meals, and using local transportation. Using the budget tips below, you can always lower this number. However, if you stay in fancier accommodation or eat out more often, expect this to be higher!)

Money Saving Tips

Get the menu of the day – Most restaurants have a cheap "menu of the day" during lunch around 7-9 EUR. They are a good way to save money on food and taste delicious Spanish food. Skip eating out for dinner — it's too expensive!

Take the bus – While the train system is fast, it's expensive. If you have the time and want to save money, take the buses.

Get city passes – Most travelers don't get city passes, but if you plan to do a lot of city sightseeing, they are a good investment. All the major cities have multiple museums, attractions, and activities. Getting a city pass can save you up to 20% on these activities and get you free transport. If you are going on a sightseeing binge, get the pass!

Couchsurf – Couchsurfing is a great way to save money on accommodation while also getting some insight from the locals. You'll have better luck in the larger cities, but be sure to request early as the major cities also see the most requests.

Camp – While Spain's rugged terrain isn't the best for camping, budget campgrounds with basic facilities can be found for as little as 15 EUR per night.

Use BlaBlaCar – A growing trend is to share rides with people. Drivers are vetted and verified and it's a much better way to get out of stuffy trains and buses, meet interesting characters, and take a mini-road trip. It's one of my preferred methods of travel. The biggest player in this space is BlaBlaCar, which is huge for getting around Europe and a couple other parts of the world.

Top Things to See and Do in Spain

Explore Madrid – The capital city is famous for its museums, tapas, and great nightlife. This is a city that doesn't start until midnight. Make sure you see the Prado, one of the largest museums in the world, and the Royal Palace. You'll also want to spend some time strolling through the main square, Plaza Mayor.

Enjoy Barcelona – Like Madrid, Barcelona is famous for its partying, late-night eating, and amazing historic streets. You'll find a lot of history here, learn to sleep until 10 pm, and eat dinner at midnight just like the locals do. I highly suggest a visit to the history museum — it is one of the best in Europe. Barcelona is one of my favorite cities in the world, and I don't doubt it's already on your list of places to see.

Revel in La Tomatina – Held the last Wednesday in August in Buñol, tens of thousands of people descend on this small town in the morning to throw tons and tons of tomatoes at each other. It was the messiest, most fun hour of traveling I've ever had. Tickets for the festival cost 10 EUR

Join the Running of the Bulls – Held in July in Pamplona, the Running of the Bulls attracts both the brave and the stupid. While I'd never do the actual running, the multi-day celebration is still a good place to go drink sangria, eat good food, wear a red scarf, and celebrate the way only Spain can.

Explore the history of Granada – This ancient Moorish city is one of my favorite in Spain. I love wandering the ancient streets in the center and relaxing in the old palace, the Alhambra. No trip to southern Spain is complete without a visit here.

Lounge on the Costa Del Sol – Come hang out on the beach and enjoy the laid-back life for which Spain is famous. The sun coast in southern Spain is famous for its beautiful beaches, great nightlife (and tons of tourists). Malaga is one of the biggest places on the coast but I think there are better places further down.

Go to Valencia – Valencia is a pretty amazing town. Initially, I wasn't attracted to Valencia for any reason in particular — I came for the tomato fight in the nearby town of Bunol, which attracts thousands of people each August, most of whom use Valencia as their home base. However, Valencia grew on me. It has great seafood, paella, history, and a good soccer team. I would go back in a second. It's a wonderful city!

Walk The Camino – El Camino de Santiago, or The Way of Saint James, is a popular pilgrimage route stretching from the border of France all the way to Santiago de Compostela in North-Western Spain. Stretching 800km, this month-long walk takes a lot of dedication. Nevertheless, it's a great way to see the country and some of the less-visited areas of Spain.

Wander through Seville – An amazing city with great churches, palaces, and historic sites. They also have good shopping here. I really like the Jewish Quarter here and the monument dedicated to the different regions of Spain. This is also a big student town.

Visit Gibraltar – Bordering Spain on the Iberian peninsula, Gibraltar is actually an overseas territory of the United Kingdom. Here you'll encounter an interesting mix of cultures, with influences from Britain, Spain, and North Africa all colliding.

Explore the islands – Whether you go to Ibiza to party or to the Canaries to relax, Spain has some of the most beautiful islands in all of Europe. Because of that, during the months of July and August, they are full and expensive so try to avoid peak season. If you love beaches, surfing, hiking, or cycling then be sure to hit up the islands (especially Gran Canaria). You won't be disappointed!

Hike in the Sierra Nevada – This mountain area is a great place for summer hiking, winter skiing, and exploring small towns. This area is one of the prettiest and most rugged in Spain and one of the better areas for outdoor activities in Spain. There are plenty of trails ranging in length and difficulty, as well as the possibility for guided tours.

Visit San Sebastián – The center of the Basque area of Spain, this place has a killer nightlife and beach. Moreover, the architecture makes it one of the most beautiful and unique cities in all of Spain.

Hike the Pyrenees – The majestic mountain chain that walls off France is laced with medieval villages, high mountain walking trails, and great skiing. It's also the traditional start of The Camino.

Visit the Great Cathedral and Mosque – The Mezquita de Cordoba is by far the most exquisite example of the Muslim fabric in Spain. Its giant arches, jasper columns, marble floors, richly gilded prayer niches, and the awe-inspiring domed shrine of Byzantine mosaics take you back to when Córdoba was under Muslim influence.

Unwind in Salamanca – Salamanca seems to be in the middle of nowhere, but it's got a huge amount of life to it. This is a university city, but it's not huge, so you can expect a mix of small-town atmosphere, great nightlife, and many backpackers.

Visit the Guggenheim Museum – One of the most famous museums in the world, the Guggenheim Museum in Bilbao always has some interesting exhibits on modern art. Even if you're not a modern art fan, you should stop by just to check it out. The architecture of this museum is something to marvel at. Frank Gehry, arguably one of the most famous living architects of today, designed it to have a very unique undulating style.

Explore Basque Country – Basque Country is an autonomous region is Spain, a place with its own unique culture and heritage. Located in the north-east corner of Spain, you'll notice the difference as soon as you step foot in the region. If you're into off-the-beaten-path locations, be sure to visit Basque Country.

When to go

If Spain is a country of many regions, it's also a country of many climates. The best time to visit depends on where you're going and what you're planning to see. The high central plains (which include Madrid) suffer from fierce extremes – stiflingly hot in summer, bitterly cold and swept by freezing winds in winter. The Atlantic coast, in contrast, has a tendency to be damp and misty, with a relatively brief, humid summer. The Mediterranean south is warm virtually all year round, and in parts of Andalucía it's positively subtropical – it's often pleasant enough to take lunch outside, even in the winter months. On a general holiday or city break, in most regions spring, the early part of summer and autumn are the best times to visit. Temperatures will be fairly clement, sites and attractions open, and tourist numbers relatively low – worth considering, especially if your destination is one of the beach resorts or cultural attractions. Spain is one of the most visited countries on the planet – it plays host to about sixty million tourists a year, rather more than the entire population – and all main tourist destinations are packed in high summer. Even the Pyrenean mountains aren't immune, swapping winter ski crowds for summer hikers and bikers. August is Spain's own holiday month – when the costas are at their most crowded, though inland cities (including Madrid) are, by contrast, pretty sleepy, since everyone who can, leaves for their annual break.

Where to go

Spain's cities are among the most vibrant in Europe. Exuberant Barcelona, for many, has the edge, thanks to Gaudí's extraordinary modernista architecture, the lively promenade of the Ramblas, five kilometres of sandy beach and the world's best football team. The capital, Madrid, may not be as pretty, but it claims as many devotees – immortalized in the movies of Pedro Almodóvar, and shot through with a contemporary style that informs everything from its major-league art museums to its carefree bars and summer cafés. Then there's Seville, home of flamenco and all the clichés of southern Spain; Valencia, the vibrant capital of the Levante, with a thriving arts scene and nightlife; and Bilbao, a not-to-miss stop on Spain's cultural circuit, due to Frank Gehry's astonishing Museo Guggenheim.

Not only are Spain's modern cities and towns lively and exciting, they are monumental – literally so. History has washed over the country, adding an architectural backdrop that varies from one region to another, dependent on their occupation by Romans, Visigoths or Moors, or on their role in the medieval Christian Reconquest or in the later Golden Age of imperial Renaissance Spain. Touring Castilla y León, for example, you can't avoid the stereotypical Spanish image of vast cathedrals and hundreds of reconquista castles, while the gorgeous medieval university city of Salamanca captivates all who visit. In northerly, mountainous Asturias and the Pyrenees, tiny, almost organically evolved, Romanesque churches dot the hillsides and villages, while in Galicia all roads lead to the ancient, and heartbreakingly beautiful cathedral city of Santiago de Compostela. Andalucía has the great mosques and Moorish palaces of Granada, Seville and Córdoba; Castilla-La Mancha boasts the superbly preserved medieval capital of Toledo; while the harsh landscape of Extremadura cradles ornate conquistador towns built with riches from the New World.

The Spanish landscape, too, holds just as much fascination and variety as the country's urban centres. The evergreen estuaries of Galicia could hardly be more different from the high, arid plains of Castile, or the gulch-like desert landscapes of Almería. In particular, Spain has some of the finest mountains in Europe, with superb walking – short hikes to week-long treks – in a dozen or more protected ranges or sierras – especially the Picos de Europa and the Pyrenees. There are still brown bears and lynx in the wild, not to mention boar, storks and eagles, while a near-five-thousand-kilometre coastline means great opportunities for fishing, whale-watching and dolphin-spotting.

Agriculture, meanwhile, makes its mark in the patterned hillsides of the wine- and olive-growing regions, the baking wheat plantations and cattle ranches of the central plains, the meseta, and the rice fields of the eastern provinces of Valencia and Murcia, known as the Levante. These areas, although short on historic monuments and attractions, produce some of Spain's most famous exports, and with the country now at the heart of the contemporary European foodie movement, there's an entire holiday to be constructed out of simply exploring Spain's rich regional cuisine – touring the Rioja and other celebrated wine regions, snacking your way around Extremadura and Andalucía in search of the world's best jamón serrano (cured mountain ham), or tucking into a paella in its spiritual home of Valencia.

And finally, there are the beaches – one of Spain's greatest attractions, and where modern tourism to the country began in the 1960s. Here, too, there's a lot more variety than the stereotypical images might suggest. Long tracts of coastline – along the Costa del Sol in Andalucía in particular – have certainly been massively and depressingly over-developed, but delightful pockets remain, even along the biggest, concrete-clad costas. Moreover, there are superb windsurfing waters around Tarifa and some decidedly low-key resorts along the Costa de la Luz. On the Costa Brava, in the northeast in Catalunya, the string of idyllic coves between Palamos and Begur is often overlooked, while the cooler Atlantic coastline boasts the surfing beaches of Cantabria and Asturias, or the unspoilt coves of Galicia's estuaries. Offshore, the Balearic Islands – Ibiza, Formentera, Mallorca and Menorca – also have some superb sands, with party-fuelled Ibiza in particular offering one of the most hedonistic backdrops to beachlife in the whole Mediterranean.

Hedonism, actually, brings us full-circle, back to one of the reasons why Spain is pretty much irresistible and infectious. Wherever you are in the country, you can't help but notice the Spaniards' wild – often over-bearing – enthusiasm for having a good time. Festival time is a case in point – these aren't staid, annual celebrations, they are raucous reaffirmations of life itself, complete with fireworks, fancy dress, giants, devils, bonfires, parties, processions and sheer Spanish glee. But even outside fiesta time there's always something vibrant and noisy happening – from local market to late-night bar, weekend football match to beachside dance club. Meals are convivial affairs – not for most Spaniards the rushed sandwich or chain-restaurant takeaway – and long lunches and late dinners are the norm throughout the country. And with family at the heart of Spanish society, there's a genuine welcome for, and interest in, you and yours, whether at resort hotel or rustic guest house. "A pasarlo bien!" (Have a good time!), as the Spanish say.

Regions

Spain is divided into autonomías or autonomous regions, plus two independent cities. Some of the autonomías - notably the ones which have other official languages alongside Spanish - are regions with their own unique historical tradition. These include the Basque Country or Euskadi (Basque), Galicia (Galician), Catalonia or Catalunya, the Valencian region or Comunitat Valenciana, and the Balearic Islands or Illes Balears (Catalan), but also Andalusia. Travelers to these parts of the Iberian Peninsula should respect their history and language. The Canary Islands lie off the coast of Morocco and are geographically part of Africa, as are the two cities of Ceuta and Melilla.

For ease of reference, Spain's many regions can be grouped as follows:

Regions of Spain

Northwestern Spain (Galicia, Asturias, Cantabria)

Northern Spain (Basque Country, Navarre, La Rioja)

Northeastern Spain (Catalonia, Aragon)

Central Spain (Community of Madrid, Castile-La Mancha, Castile-Leon, Extremadura)

Eastern Spain (Murcia, Valencia)

Andalusia

Balearic Islands

Canary Islands

Autonomous Cities (Ceuta, Melilla)

Cities

Spain has hundreds of interesting cities. Here are ten of the most popular:

Madrid — the vibrant capital, with fantastic museums, interesting architecure, great food and nightlife

Barcelona — Spain's second city, full of modernist buildings and a vibrant cultural life, nightclubs, and beaches

Bilbao — industrial city, home to the Guggenheim Museum

Cadiz — oldest city in Western Europe with nearly 4,000 years of history, celebrates a famous carnival

Cordoba — The Grand Mosque ('Mezquita') of Cordoba is one of the world's finest buildings

Granada — stunning city in the south, surrounded by snow capped mountains of the Sierra Nevada, home of La Alhambra

Seville — a beautiful, verdant city, and home to the world's third largest cathedral

Valencia — paella was invented here, has a very nice beach

Zaragoza — fifth largest city of Spain that held the World Expo in 2008

Other destinations

Costa Blanca — 200 km of white coast with plenty of beaches and small villages

Costa Brava — the rugged coast with plenty of seaside resorts

Costa del Sol — the sunny coast in the south of the country

Gran Canaria — known as "a continent in miniature" due to its many different climates and landscapes

Ibiza — a Balearic island; one of the best places for clubbing, raving, and DJs in the entire world

La Rioja — Rioja wine and fossilized dinosaur tracks

Mallorca — the largest island of the Balears, full of amazing beaches and great nightlife

Sierra Nevada — the highest mountains on the Iberian Peninsula, great for walking and skiing

Tenerife — offers lush forests, exotic fauna and flora, deserts, mountains, volcanoes, beautiful coastlines and spectacular beaches

Get in

Entry requirements

Minimum validity of travel documents

EU, EEA and Swiss citizens, need only produce a passport or national identity card which is valid on the date of entry.

Other nationals must produce a passport which is valid for the entirety of their period of stay in Spain.

More information about the minimum validity of travel documents is available at this webpage of the Ministry of Foreign Affairs and Cooperation of Spain.

Spain is a member of the Schengen Agreement.

There are no border controls between countries that have signed and implemented this treaty - the European Union (except Bulgaria, Croatia, Cyprus, Ireland, Romania and the United Kingdom), Iceland, Liechtenstein, Norway and Switzerland. Likewise, a visa granted for any Schengen member is valid in all other countries that have signed and implemented the treaty. But be careful: not all EU members have signed the Schengen treaty, and not all Schengen members are part of the European Union. This means that there may be spot customs checks but no immigration checks (travelling within Schengen but to/from a non-EU country) or you may have to clear immigration but not customs (travelling within the EU but to/from a non-Schengen country).

Please see the article Travel in the Schengen Zone for more information about how the scheme works and what entry requirements are.

EU, EEA and Swiss nationals who enter Spain on a national identity card, who are under 18 years old and travelling without their parents are required to have written parental consent. For more information, visit this webpage of the Ministry of Foreign Affairs and Cooperation of Spain.

Citizens of Antigua and Barbuda, the Bahamas, Barbados, Mauritius, Saint Kitts and Nevis and Seychelles are permitted to work in Spain without the need to obtain a visa or any further authorisation for the period of their 90 day visa-free stay. However, this ability to work visa-free does not necessarily extend to other Schengen countries.

When entering by air from a non-Schengen country, you will be expected to fill out a brief form which includes an address in Spain, such as a hotel or hostel. This does not appear to be stringently checked, but you will not be allowed in unless an address has been entered.

A stay of longer than 90 days for non-EEA or Swiss citizens almost invariably requires an advance visa. If one stays for longer than 6 months, a residence permit (Titulo de Residencia) must be obtained within the first 30 days of entering Spain.

There are a number of ways to get into Spain. From neighbouring European countries, a drive with the car or a train ride is feasible; visitors from further away will probably be using air travel.

By plane

Spain's national carrier is Iberia.

The busiest airports are Madrid, Barcelona, Palma de Mallorca and Malaga, followed by Seville, Valencia, Bilbao, Alicante, Santiago de Compostela, Vigo, Gran Canaria and the 2 airports in Tenerife. All are listed on the official airport governing body website:

Madrid, Barcelona and Bilbao have the most beautiful airports, designed by famous architects.

Low cost carriers operating to Spain include: Vueling, easyJet, Ryanair, Blue Air, and Jet2.com.

Warning: If you buy an e-ticket from Iberia over the internet with a credit card, you may have to show the original credit card upon check-in. If you fail to do so, you will have to purchase another ticket for the same fare, and the original ticket will be refunded many weeks or even months later.

By train

The best option to arrive in Spain by train is the high-speed track from France, connecting Paris with Barcelona and further with Madrid. It takes 6 hours of travel from Paris to Barcelona. Cross-border connections are also frequent on the other end of the border with France, between San Sebastian and Bayonne. A more scenic option is to from Toulouse to Barcelona is the regional train TER from Toulouse to Latour-de-Carol, on the border, connecting with a regional spanish train to Barcelona.

Trains from Portugal are slow and not so frequent.

By bus

Bus travel in Spain is increasingly an attractive option for people traveling on a tight budget.

There are lots of private bus companies offering routes to all major Spanish cities. If you want to travel around Spain by bus, the best idea is to go to your local bus station (Apart from Madrid and Barcelona, most towns and cities have just one) and see what is available.

Traveling by bus in Spain is usually reliable (except on peak holiday days when roads can be very crowded and you should expect long delays on popular routes), coaches are modern and comfortable. You can expect to pay about €8 per 100km.

By boat

From the UK, Brittany Ferries offers services from Portsmouth and Plymouth to Santander and from Portsmouth to Bilbao. The journey time from Portsmouth to Santander is approximately 24 hours.

Ferry services were once run by P&O from Portsmouth to Bilbao and from Plymouth and Southampton to Santander. However, P&O no longer operates these routes.

As well as the UK, Spain is also well connected by Ferry to Northern Africa (particularly Algeria and Morocco) and the Canary Islands which are owned by Spain. Routes are also naturally available to the Spanish Balearic islands of Mallorca, Minorca, Ibiza and Formentera.

Another popular route is from Barcelona to Genoa.

Spain Yatching Group S.L. Yacht charter and sailing - INTERNATIONAL YACHTING GROUP, one of the worlds largest yacht charter companies, can take care of all charter requirements, from bareboat to crewed in Spain and Wordwide.

Visas

Spain is a member of the European Union and the Schengen Agreement, which governs its visa policies. No visa is required for citizens of other EU member states, and those of nations with whom the European Union has special treaties. There are no border controls between Spain and other Schengen Agreement nations, making travel less complicated.

As of May 2004 citizens of the following countries do not need a visa for entry into Spain. Note that citizens of these countries (except EU nationals) must not stay longer than three months in any 180 day period in any country covered by the Schengen Agreement and they must not work in Spain: Andorra, Argentina, Australia, Austria, Belgium, Bermuda, Bolivia, Brazil, Brunei, Bulgaria, Canada, Chile, Costa Rica, Croatia, Cyprus, Czech Republic, Denmark, El Salvador, Estonia, Finland, France, Greece, Guatemala, Honduras, Hong Kong, Hungary, Iceland, Ireland, Israel, Italy, Japan, Latvia, Liechtenstein, Lithuania, Luxembourg, Macao, Malaysia, Malta, Mexico, Monaco, New Zealand, Netherlands, Nicaragua, Norway, Panama, Paraguay, Poland, Portugal, Romania, San Marino, Singapore, Slovakia, Slovenia, South Korea, Spain, Sweden, Switzerland, United Kingdom, United States, Uruguay, Vatican City and Venezuela.

For Latin American people, especially those from Bolivia, Colombia, Ecuador, Peru, Paraguay, Argentina, Chile, and Venezuela, you need to have a hotel reservation confirmed, and international insurance for at least 30.000 EURO; if your trip is from 1-9 days you need €514, for each additional day €57 and a return air ticket.

Venezuelan credit cards are not accepted like funds for immigration due to the currency exchange control in this country.

Get around

By train

RENFE is the Spanish national rail carrier. Long-distance trains always get in time, but be aware that short-distance trains (called Cercanías) can bear long delays, from ten to twenty minutes, and especially in the Barcelona area, where delays up to 30 minutes are not uncommon. To be safe, always take the train before the one you need.

Trains and facilities are clean, services are fast and reliable and Prices are on par with those found elsewhere in Western Europe, but there is one catch. Since absolutely all long-distance trains require a reservation (not only the high-speed AVEs!) and are booked out long before, especially in the tourist season, getting around Spain by train is rather difficult and planning ahead is essential. If you turn up at the Madrid-Atocha station expecting to buy a same-day AVE ticket to Barcelona or to the costas, you'll be disappointed. On the other hand, passengers in Spain ride in style, everyone seated and no people standing in the aisle. This is in sharp contrast with most other European countries, where compulsory reservations are either non-existent or only required for the highest category of trains.

FEVE

Narrow-gauge, slow, but scenic trains around the northern coast of Spain are operated by another company, FEVE. These trains are a completely separate ecosystem. They require different tickets and are not covered by Rail Passes! The FEVE company was formally merged with RENFE on January 1, 2013, but it'll take some more time until the factual merger completes.

If you'd like to travel by trains, you have the following choices:

Buy tickets in advance through the RENFE website. They can be significantly cheaper when bought a long time ahead. Fortunately, the RENFE website has seen some major improvements in the recent years, especially its English version, which used to be severely limited. A RENFE ticket can only be bought for a specified train and date. Best Price can be achieved by buying approx. one month in advance (of course, discounted tickets are non-refundable). Beware though, that you cannot buy a separate seat reservation without a ticket (if you're travelling on a rail pass) on the Renfe website. That can be bought easily in Spain at a railway station, but by the time you get into Spain, the train will likely be booked out. It is technically possible to buy Spanish seat reservations (including domestic routest) everywhere in Europe, at any train station selling international tickets, since the railway companies are interconnected, but it's not easy. Imagine explaining to a ticket selling person in, say, Germany or Poland that you want to buy a reservation for a train in Spain! That being said, it is nonetheless possible. Always give the train number (very important!), exact date, departure and arrival points. With these information, buying a reservation abroad should succeed. Alternately, you can buy a seat reservation on the RailDude website. It is a bit more expensive (€10 for a 2nd class reservation), but you'll avoid haggling with railway staff and it is your best option if you're outside Europe.

Travel only by local trains (Cercanías - suburban trains, or Media Distancia - medium distance trains). Sadly, quite a lot of the Media Distancia trains are subject to compulsory reservations, too. Always check for each connection whether you require a reservation or not. There are e.g. only 7 daily trains between Santiago de Compostela and A Coruña (a relatively short way) which don't require a reservation. All other trains on that route (29 more trains) require a reservation, either being Media Distancia or Larga Distancia (long-distance services). Anyway, the main difference is that the Media Distancia trains do not tend to be booked out weeks before so it is usually possible to buy a reservation minutes before your desired departure.

CAVEAT: The RENFE website only accepts those foreign-issued credit cards which have a 2-Step Verification System like those issued by Indian Banks so it will not accept US Banks issued Credit Cards. If however the transaction fails, you can contact your bank, but don't expect a solution. Use a PayPal account instead, or pay about 10 Euros more to buy your ticket from a travel agent.

These facts turn travelling by train in Spain into a nightmare for rail pass holders, and into (at least) a mild nuisance for other travellers. Even young Spaniards don't travel long distances by train very often. They usually ride a bus (when they're on a tight budget or have to travel on a short notice) or fly (when they can book in advance). Flights within Spain are not much more expensive than trains and are well worth looking into, because of the time you save. Just keep in mind that the AVE high-speed train service between Madrid and Barcelona is actually faster than taking a plane, when you factor in all airport transfers and security checks! On the other hand, trains are more comfortable and allow you to take plenty of luggage.

By bus

The easiest way to get around most parts of Spain is by bus. Most major routes are point to point, and very high frequency. There is a different operator for each route, but usually just one operator per route. At the bus station, each operator has its own ticket. The staff at any of them is usually happy to tell you who operates which route. The following two are major bus companies serving much of the country:

Grupo Alsa, Avenida de América Intercambiador 9-A, 28002 Madrid, ☎ +34 902 42 22 42, which also included Continental Auto

Grupo Avanza, ☎ +34 91 272 28 32, operates the Alosa, Tusza, Vitrasa & Auto Res lines

... or see Movelia.es (an independent bus booking site) for additional smaller bus lines serving specific autonomous regions or provinces in the country or see the article(s) on a specific city, town, province or autonomous community as to what's there.

By boat

Wherever you are in Spain, from your private yacht you can enjoy gorgeous scenery and distance yourself from the inevitable crowds of tourists that flock to these destinations. May is a particularly pleasant time to charter in the regions of Costa Brava, Costa Blanca and the Balearic Islands as the weather is good and the crowds have yet to descend. The summer months of July and August are the hottest and tend to have lighter winds. There is no low season for the Canary Islands, as the weather resembles springtime all year round. If you would like to bareboat anywhere in Spain, including the Balearic or Canary Islands, a US Coast Guard License is the only acceptable certification needed by Americans to bareboat. For everyone else, a RYA Yacht Master Certification or International Certificate of Competence will normally do. Although a skipper may be required, a hostess/chef may or may not be necessary. Dining out is strong part of Spanish custom and tradition. If you are planning on docking in a port and exploring fabulous bars and restaurants a hostess/cook may just be useful for serving drinks and making beds. Extra crew can take up valuable room on a tight ship.

Yacht and boats rentals in Spain, - Costa Brava, Costa Central, Costa Daurada, Majorca, Minorca, Ibiza and Formentera.

Luxury yachts in Spain, - Yacht charter and sailing, one of the worlds largest acht charter companies, can take care of all charter requirements, from bareboat to crewed in Spain. Operating from nine offices worldwide (USA, Spain, UK, Germany, Italy, France, Spain, Switzerland, Caribbean, Hong Kong and Dubai)

By car

In major cities like Madrid or Barcelona and in mid-sized ones like San Sebastian, moving around by car is both expensive and nerve-wracking. Fines for improper parking are uncompromising (€85 and up).

Having a driving map is essential - many streets are one-way; left turns are more rare than rights (and are unpredictable).

Getting around by car makes sense if you plan to move from one city to another every other day, ideally if you don't plan to park overnight in large cities. It also doesn't hurt that the scenery is beautiful and well worth a drive.

There are two types of highway in Spain: autopistas, or motorways, and autovías, which are more akin to expressways. Most autopistas are toll roads while autovías are generally free of charge. Speed limits range from 50 km/h in towns to 90 km/h on rural roads, 100 km/h on roads and 120 km/h on autopistas and autovías.

Intersections of two highways typically have a roundabout under the higher one – so you can both choose any turn and to start driving in an opposite direction there.

Green light for cars about to turn is frequently on at the same time as green light for pedestrians: every time you turn, check if the pedestrians' path you cross doesn't also have green light for them.

Between cities, profesional drivers (bus drivers for example) are required to have some rest every 2 hours they drive--there's a fine if you don't follow.

Filling procedure for gas stations varies from brand to brand. At Agip, you first fill the tank yourself, and then pay inside the shop. Gasoline is relatively inexpensive compared to other countries in the EU and Japan, but still more expensive than in the U.S.

Speed Limits:

Usually, maximum speed limits are as follows: Motorways - 120 km/h; Fast main roads – 100 km/h; Other non-urban roads – 90 km/h; Urban towns and cities – 50 km/h.

The minimum speed allowed on motorways is 60 km/h. Be observant! Some residential roads in Spain have lower speed limits – even 20 km/h.

Luckily, all speed limits are adequately indicated on large warning signs in their locations.

Speeding fines (multas) are high in Spain and depend on the degree to which you exceed the speed limit. On-the-spot fines can reach 600 EUR. Speeding fines must be paid within 60 days. If you pay your fine within a certain amount of time, you may get up to 50% discount. Spanish police use numerous static speed cameras and portable radar traps. Static cameras are mainly set on the 120 km/h motorways. They can be occasionally painted in fluorescent yellow with a speed limit on them.

By thumb

Spain isn't a good country for hitchhiking. Sometimes you can wait many hours. Try to speak with people at gas stations, parking lots etc. They are scared and suspicious, but when you show them that they shouldn't be afraid, they gladly accept you and mostly also show their generosity. In the South of Spain, in and around the Alpujarras, hitchhiking is very common and it is also very easy to get a ride. As long as you can speak a bit of spanish and don't look too dirty/frightening, you should be able to get a ride moderately easily.

Renting a car

If you plan to move around large cities or explore further afield you will find many companies that offer car hire at affordable Prices because of the high competition between car rental agencies, consider renting a car with GPS navigation--it will be even easier to drive than having an automobile map.

Consider having full-coverage insurance instead of franchise: other drivers are not always careful parking near other cars, especially when parking space on a street is limited.

Spanish drivers can be unpredictable and some of the roads on the Southern area of Malaga and the Costa Del Sol are notoriously dangerous.

Therefore you will want a car with a fully comprehensive insurance package with includes a collision damage waiver (CDW) and a vehicle theft waiver, as well as liability cover. Many of the car hire companies offer an insurance option where you can choose to reduce your vehicle excess. This means that if you are in an accident you would not be financially liable for the whole excess fee.

Child seats are also available with all vehicles so that any children in your party can travel safely and in comfort.

Air conditioning is a must in the hot Spanish summer months. Nevertheless you should make sure to take water with you at all times.

If you break down while on holiday you will want a car hire company that gives you the free roadside assistance of trained mechanics. Cars often overheat in Spain while the tires are vulnerable on the hot roads.

Avis accepts payment in US dollars when you pay by a credit card. If you need to pay when you return rented car, payment is made from deposit you provided by credit card in the beginning--so you don't pay extra money upon return, waiting for weeks for deposit to be unblocked. link Sixt in Spain is one of the biggest car rental companies in Spain where you will be able to get a rent a car no matter what city you are in Spain.

By bicycle

Spain is heaven for cycling, judging by how many cyclists you can see in the cities. Cycling lanes are available in mid-sized and large cities. It must be taken into account that Spain is the second most mountainous country in Europe, and the mountains and hills are from coast to coast. For example, Madrid is between 600 and 700 metres above sea, so if you travel through it by bicycle you have to be in a good shape.

By taxi

All the major cities in Spain are served by taxis, which are a convenient, if somewhat expensive way to get around. That being said, taxis in Spain are more reasonably Priced than those in say, the United Kingdom or Japan. Most taxi drivers do not speak English or any other foreign languages, so it would be necessary to have the names and/or addresses of your destinations written in Spanish to show your taxi driver. Likewise, get your hotel's business card to show your taxi driver in case you get lost.

Talk

Many English words have their origins in Latin, which makes it easy for English speakers to guess the meanings of many Spanish words. However, Spanish and English also have a number of false cognates that one needs to be aware of to avoid embarrassing mistakes.

embarazada - pregnant; not embarrassed

suburbio - slum; not suburb

preservativo - condom; not preservative

bizarro - brave; not bizarre

Unsurprisingly, the official and universal language used in Spain is Spanish (español), but it is more complicated than that. It is part of the Romance family of languages (others include Portuguese, Galician, Catalan, Italian, Occitan, French, and Romanian) and is one of the main branches of that family. Many people, especially outside Castille, prefer to call it Castilian (castellano).

However, there are a number of languages (Catalan, Basque, Galician, Asturian, etc.) spoken in various parts of Spain. Some of these languages are dominant in their respective regions, and, following their legalization in the 1978 constitution, they are co-official with Castilian in their respective areas. Of these, Catalan, Basque and Galician are recognised as official languages according to the Spanish constitution. In the Basque Country and Catalonia, Spanish is more widely spoken than Basque and Catalan, but the regional governments try and encourage the use of both languages in their respective regions. Apart from Basque (whose origins are still debated), the languages of the Iberian Peninsula are part of the Romance family and are fairly easy to pick up if you know Castilian well. While locals in those also speak Spanish fluently, learning a few words in the local languages where you are traveling will help endear you to the locals. Galician is the only language which has a native majority in its region. All Spaniards are functionally bilingual and no-one should have problems communicating in Spanish.

Catalan (Catalan: català, Castilian: catalán), a distinct language similar to Castilian but more closely related to the Oc branch of the Romance Languages and considered by many to be part of a dialect continuum spanning across Spain, France, and Italy and including the other langues d'oc such as Provençal, Beàrnais, Limousin, Auvernhat and Niçard. Various dialects are spoken in the northeastern region of Catalonia, the Balearic Islands, and Valencia (where it is often referred to as Valencià), east of Aragon, as well as neighboring Andorra and southern France. To a casual listener, Catalan superficially appears to be a cross of Castilian and French, and though it does share features of both, it is an independent language in its own right.

Galician (Galician: galego, Castilian: gallego), very closely related to Portuguese, Galician is spoken in Galicia and the western portion of Asturias. Galician predates Portuguese and is deemed one of the four main dialects of the Galician-Portuguese family group which includes Brazilian, Southern Portuguese, Central Portuguese, and Galician. While some Portuguese might consider it a dialect of Portuguese, Galicians themselves consider it their own language.

Basque (Basque: euskara, Castilian: vasco), a language unrelated to Castilian (or any other known language in the world), is spoken in the three provinces of the Basque Country, on the two adjacent provinces on the French side of the Spain-French border, and in Navarre. Basque is unrelated to any Romance language or to any branch of the Indo-European family of languages. It currently remains unclassified and is deemed a linguistic isolate.

Asturiano (Asturiano: asturianu, Castilian: asturiano, also known as bable), spoken in the province of Asturias, where it enjoys semi-official protection. It was also spoken in rural parts of Leon, Zamora, Salamanca, in a few villages in Portugal (where it is called Mirandes) and in villages in the extreme north of Extremadura. While the constitution of Spain explicitly protects Basque, Balearic-Catalan-Valencian under the term Catalan, Galician, and Castilian, it does not explicitly protect Asturian. Still, the province of Asturias explicitly protects it, and Spain implicitly protects it by not objecting before the Supreme Court.

Aragonese (Aragonese: aragonés, Castilian: aragonés, also known colloquially as fabla), spoken in the north of Aragon. It is only vaguely recognized and not official (as of June 2008). This language is close to Catalan (specially in Benasque) and to Castilian, with some Basque and Occitan (southern France) influences. Nowadays, only a few villages near the Pyrenees use the language vigorously, while most people mix it with Castilian in their daily speech.

Aranese (Castilian: Aranés, Catalan/Aranese Occitan: Aranès), spoken in the Aran Valley and recognized as an official language of Catalonia (not of Spain), alongside Catalan and Castilian. This language is a variety of Gascon Occitan, and as such is very closely related to Provençal, Limousin, Languedoc, and Catalan.

In addition to the native languages, English and French are commonly studied in school. While most younger Spaniards have studied English in school, due to a lack of practice and exposure, proficiency is generally poor, and most people will not know more than a few basic words. If you are lost, your best bet would generally be young urban people. To improve your chances of being understood, stick to simple words and avoid long sentences.

That being said, airlines, major hotels and popular tourist destinations usually have staff members who speak an acceptable level of English, and particularly in popular beach resorts such as those in the Costa del Sol, you will find people who are fluent in several languages. English is also generally more widely spoken in Barcelona than in the rest of the country. As Portuguese and Italian are closely related to Spanish, if you speak either of these languages, locals would be able to puzzle you out with some difficulty, and as long as you speak slowly, you won't need an interpreter for the most part.

Castillian Spanish differs from the Latin American varieties in pronunciation and other details. There is also a pronoun ("vosotros", literally "you others", used to address a group of two or more people in the second person) and its associated verb conjugations, rarely used in Latin American Spanish. However, all Latin American varieties are easily understood by Spaniards, and are recognized simply as different versions of one language by the Royal Spanish Academy, the barometer for all things Spanish language. While some Spaniards believe theirs is the more 'pure' version of Spanish, most Spaniards recognize the reality that there is no 'pure' Spanish, even within their own country.

French is the most widely understood foreign language in the northeast of Spain, like Alquezar and Cap de Creus (at times even better than English), as most travelers there come from France.

Locals will appreciate any attempts you make to speak their language. For example, know at least the Castilian for "good morning" (buenos días) and "thank you" (gracias).

See

The most popular beaches are the ones in the Mediterranean coasts and the Canary Islands. Meanwhile, for hiking, the mountains of Sierra Nevada in the south, the Central Cordillera and the northern Pyrenees are the best places.

Itineraries

Via de la Plata Route Historic 800km route from Gijón to Sevilla.

Way of St. James

Historic cities

Historically, Spain has been an important crossroads: between the Mediterranean and the Atlantic, between North Africa and Europe, and as Europe beginning colonizing the New World, between Europe and the Americas. As such, the country is blessed with a fantastic collection of historical landmarks - in fact, it has the 2nd largest number of UNESCO

Heritage Sites and the largest number of World Heritage Cities of any nation in the world.

In the south of Spain, Andalusia holds many reminders of old Spain. Cadiz is regarded as one of the oldest continuously-inhabited cities in western Europe, with remnants of the Roman settlement that once stood here. Nearby, Ronda is a beautiful town situated atop steep cliffs and noted for its gorge-spanning bridge and the oldest bullring in Spain. Cordoba and Granada hold the most spectacular reminders of the nation's Muslim past, with the red-and-white striped arches of the Mezquita in Cordoba and the stunning Alhambra palace perched on a hill above Granada. Seville, the cultural center of Andalusia, has dazzling collections of sights built when the city was the main port for goods from the Americas, the grandest of which being the city's cathedral, the largest in the country.

Moving north across the plains of La Mancha into Central Spain, picturesque Toledo stands as perhaps the historical center of the nation, a beautiful medieval city sitting atop a hill that once served as the capital of Spain before Madrid was built. Not far from the Portuguese border, Merida contains well preserved Roman ruins, a UNESCO World Heritage site. North of Madrid and an easy day-trip from the capital city is El Escorial, once the center of the Spanish empire during the time of the Inquisition; Segovia, noted for its spectacular Roman aqueduct which spans one of the city's squares; and the beautiful walled city of Avila. Further north, culture tourists will enjoy Burgos, with its beautiful Gothic cathedral and the world famous archaeological site of Atapuerca; Leon, whose Gothic cathedral was the first national protected building; Salamanca, known for its famous university and abundance of historic architecture; and Soria, with the nearby pre-roman archaeological site of Numancia.

Galicia in northwestern Spain is home to Santiago de Compostela, the end point of the old Way of St. James (Camino de Santiago) pilgrimage route and the supposed burial place of St. James, with perhaps the most beautiful cathedral in all of Spain at the heart of its lovely old town. Northeastern Spain has a couple of historical centers to note: Zaragoza, with Roman, Muslim, medieval and Renaissance buildings from throughout its two thousand years of history, and Barcelona with its medieval Barri Gòtic neighborhood.

Visitors should be aware of the limited hours and likely entrance fees at many historic Spanish churches. With entry fees averaging €8, families will need to take the expense of religious sightseeing in Spain into account. Another important consideration when planning your trip to Spain are the limited hours of access to Spanish churches. Unlike neighbouring countries Italy, France and Germany, churches in Spain are only open for mass once or twice a day and thus, only open to the local worshipping population. While large cathedrals are open all day, these only represent some of the significant christian legacy of Spain. When combined with the high entry Prices and bans on photography levied against you to visit most of the large cathedrals of the country, a trip to Spain to indulge yourself in Christian history can be challenging.

Art museums

Spain has played a key role in Western art, heavily influenced by French and Italian artists but very distinct in its own regard, owing to the nation's history of Muslim influence, Counter-Reformation climate and, later, the hardships from the decline of the Spanish empire, giving rise to such noted artists like El Greco, Diego Velázquez and Francisco Goya. In the last century, Spain's unique position in Europe brought forth some of the leading artists of the Modernist and Surrealist movements, most notably the famed Picasso and Salvador Dalí.

Today, Spain's two largest cities hold the lion's share of Spain's most famous artworks. Madrid's Museum Triangle is home to the Museo del Prado, the largest art museum in Spain with many of the most famous works by El Greco, Velázquez, and Goya as well as some notable works by Italian, Flemish, Dutch and German masters. Nearby sits the Reina Sofía, most notable for holding Picasso's Guernica but also containing a number of works by Dalí and other Modernist, Surrealist and abstract painters.

Barcelona is renowned for its stunning collection of modern and contemporary art and architecture. This is where you will find the Picasso Museum, which covers the artist's early career quite well, and the architectural wonders of Antoni Gaudi, with their twisting organic forms that are a delight to look at. A day trip from Barcelona is the town of Figueres, noted for the Salvador Dalí Museum, designed by the Surrealist himself.

Outside of Madrid and Barcelona, the art museums quickly dwindle in size and importance, although there are a couple of worthy mentions that should not be looked over: Many of El Greco's most famous works lie in Toledo, an easy day trip from Madrid. The Disrobing of Christ, perhaps El Greco's most famous work, sits in the Cathedral, but you can also find work by him in one of the small art museums around town. Valladolid is home to the National Museum of Sculpture, with an extensive collection ranging from the Middle Ages to the 19th century. Bilbao in the Basque Country of northern Spain is home to a spectacular Guggenheim Museum designed by Frank Gehry that has put the city on the map.

Besides the public museums, you will also find some contemporary art treasures in private galleries. A directory containing a major part of them is available at Consorcio De Galerias.

Do

Festivals

Spain has a lot of local festivals that are worth going to.

Feria de Abril (Sevilla in April/May) - Best fair in the whole Iberian peninsula that attracts thousands of people from all over the world. If you enjoy folklore, flamenco, dancing and drinking, this is your place.

Sevilla's & Málaga's Semana Santa (Easter) - worth seeing. From Palm Sunday to Easter Sunday. Lots of processions occur within that week. Holy week (Easter Week) - best in Seville and the rest of Andalusia; also interesting in Valladolid (silent processions) and Zaragoza (where hundreds of drums are played in processions)

Córdoba en Mayo (Cordoba in May) - great month to visit the Southern city

Las Cruces (1st week in May) - big flower-made crosses embellishing public squares in the city center, where you will also find at night music and drinking and lot of people having fun!

Festival de Patios - one of the most interesting cultural exhibitions, 2 weeks when some people open doors of their houses to show their old Patios full of flowers

Arde Lucus - biggest roman recreation festival of Europe, all inside the walled city of Lugo, UNESCO World Heritage. Last weekend on June.

Cata del Vino Montilla-Moriles - great wine tasting in a big tent in the city center during one week in May

Dia de Sant Jordi - The Catalan must, in April 23th Barcelona is embellished with roses everywhere and book-selling stands can be found in the Rambla. There are also book signings, concerts and diverse animations.

Fallas - Valencia's festival in March - burning the "fallas" is a must

Málaga's August Fair - flamenco dancing, drinking sherry, bullfights

San Fermines - July in Pamplona, Navarra.

Fiesta de San Isidro - May 15 in Madrid - a celebration of Madrid's patron saint.

Carnival - best in Santa Cruz de Tenerife, Las Palmas de Gran Canaria and Cádiz

Cabalgata de los Reyes Magos (Three wise men parade) - on the eve of epiphany, 5th of January, the night before Spanish kids get their Christmas presents, it rains sweets and toys in every single town and city

San Sebastian International Film Festival - held annually in San Sebastian, a gorgeous city in the Basque Country, towards the end of September

La Tomatina - a giant tomato fight in Buñol

Moros y Cristianos (Moors and Christians, mostly found in Southeastern Spain during spring time) - parades and "battles" remembering the fights of medieval ages

85 festivals in Galicia throughout the year from wine to wild horses.

Holidays

New Year's Eve: There's a tradition in Spain to eat grapes as the clock counts down the New Year, one grape for each of the last twelve seconds before midnight. For this, even small packs of grapes (exactly 12 grapes per pack) are sold in supermarkets before New Year.

Outdoor activities

Vías Verdes in: Cycling from the Pyrinees to the Mediterranean Coast: a weekend getaway

This is an experience that combines nature and sport, has 2 contrasting landscapes: the mountainous Pyrenees and the Mediterranean Costa Brava, goes off-the-beaten-track places where few tourists and foreigners go, offers delicious inland Catalan food and finishes by with a swim in the Mediterranean and eating Mediterranean food. Green-Ways, also known as Vías Verdes in Spanish, are old railway tracks that have been recovered and reconditioned for walkers and cyclists. They are an awesome way to discover Spain. They are easy to access and since trains once rolled over these paths, there is no So it is a great activity for all ages and fitness levels. There are 1,800 kilometres of Vías Verdes all over Spain. There is easy access to Vías Verdes by train. In total, there would be 138 km of cycling for one weekend. The trip starts in the Pyrenees and finishes in the beaches of Costa Brava. Until Girona the landscapes are mountaineous, green, wet and you can feel real nature. You cross small villages and rivers. After Girona the towns become larger and there are some parts that look more industrialized. But as you approach to the end, in Sant Feliu de Guíxols, the scenery becomes more Mediterranean and you start smelling the pine trees and for sure the sea. The hardest part of the trip is climbing to the coll of Santigosa (hill of Santigosa). Along the way there are plenty of opportunities to stay at rural homes and truly experience local living. If you are interested in a trip like this contact: www.spainforreal.com

For more information about Catalan Green-Ways you can look here: http://www.viasverdes.com/en/principal.asp

Canyoning: see Spain section in the Canyoning article

Climbing in: Los Mallos (Aragon) and Siurana (near Barcelona)

Whitewater sports in: Campo, Murillo de Gallego (Aragon)

Hiking in Galicia

Downhill skiing There are a lot of downhill skiing resorts in Spain.

Skiing in the northen region of Spain

Scuba Diving

For a treat, try Costa Brava and the world renowned Canary Islands.

Buy

Spain has the euro (€) as its sole currency along with 24 other countries that use this common European money. These 24 countries are: Austria, Belgium, Cyprus, Estonia, Finland, France, Germany, Greece, Ireland, Italy, Latvia, Lithuania, Luxembourg, Malta, the Netherlands, Portugal, Slovakia, Slovenia and Spain (official euro members which are all European Union member states) as well as Andorra, Kosovo, Monaco, Montenegro, San Marino and the Vatican which use it without having a say in eurozone affairs and without being European Union members. Together, these countries have a population of more than 330 million.

One euro is divided into 100 cents. While each official euro member (as well as Monaco, San Marino and Vatican) issues its own coins with a unique obverse, the reverse, as well as all bank notes, look the same throughout the eurozone. Every coin is legal tender in any of the eurozone countries.

The euro replaced the Spanish peseta in 2002. A few people may still use the old national currency (166,386 pts = 1 €, 1.000 pts = 6 €) and convert into Euros later. This is much due to the huge presence of peseta, and "her" many nicknames in colloquial Spanish.

Cash euro: €500 banknotes are not accepted in many stores--always have alternative banknotes.

Other currencies: Do not expect anybody to accept other types of currency, or to be willing to exchange currency. Exceptions are shops and restaurants at airports. These will generally accept at least US Dollars at a slightly worse exchange rate.

If you wish to exchange money, you can do so at any bank (some may require that you have an account there before they will exchange your money), where you can also cash in your traveller's cheques. Currency exchanges, once a common sight, have all but disappeared since the introduction of the Euro. Again, international airports are an exception to this rule; other exception is tourist districts in the large cities (Barcelona, Madrid).

Credit cards: Credit cards are well accepted: even in a stall at La Boqueria market in Barcelona, on an average highway gas station in the middle of the country, or in small towns like Alquezar. It's more difficult to find a place where credit card is not accepted in Spain.

Most ATMs will allow you to withdraw money with your credit card, but you'll need to know your card's PIN for that. Most Spanish stores will ask for ID before accepting your credit card. Some stores may not accept a foreign driving license or ID card and you will need to show your passport. This measure is designed to help avoid credit card fraud.

Business hours

Most businesses (including most shops, but not restaurants) close in the afternoons around 13:30/14:00 and reopen for the evening around 16:30/17:00. Exceptions are large malls or major chain stores.

For most Spaniards, lunch is the main meal of the day and you will find bars and restaurants open during this time. On Saturdays, businesses often do not reopen in the evening and almost everywhere is closed on Sundays. The exception is the month of December, where most shops in Madrid and Barcelona will be open as per on weekdays on Sundays to cash in on the festive season. Also, many public offices and banks do not reopen in the evenings even on weekdays, so if you have any important business to take care of, be sure to check hours of operation.

If you plan to spend whole day shopping in small shops, the following rule of thumb can work: a closed shop should remind it's also time for your own lunch. And when you finish your lunch, some shops will be likely open again.

Clothes and shoes

Designer brands

Besides well-known mass brands which are known around the world (Zara, Mango, Bershka, Camper, Desigual), Spain has many designer brands which are more hard to find outside Spain--and may be worth looking for if you shop for designer wear while travelling. Some of these brands include:

Custo Barcelona, Headquartered in Barcelona, has stores in Bilbao, Ibiza, La Coruna, Las Palmas de Gran Canaria, Leon, Madrid, Marbella, Palma de Mallorca, Salamanca, Tenerife.

Kowalski, head office: Ctra. del Leon, km, 2; 03293 Elche, ☎ +34 966 630 612, Designer shoes and sneakers (trademark Herman Monster and others) for women, men and unisex.

Department stores

El Corte Ingles, Major national chain that can be found in nearly every city. In most cities, enjoys central location but resides in functional, uninspiring buildings. Has department for everything--but is not good enough for most purposes, except maybe for buying gourmet food and local food specialties. Still very popular with uneducated travelling shoppers - the locals consider it expensive for a department store, though its customer service is well regarded. Tax refund for purchases at El Corte Ingles, unlike most other stores in Spain, can be returned only to a debit/credit card, even if you originally paid in cash. Also, given that they usually occupy very large buildings, Corte Ingles stores are usually a landmark in major Spanish cities and are very well connected to the local mass transit networks.

Others

Casas. A chain of footwear stores that selects most popular (?) models from a dozen+ of mid-range brands.

Camper, Camper shoes can be seen in most cities in the country. While it may seem that they are sold everywhere, finding right model and size may be a trouble--so if you find what you need, don't postpone your purchase. Campers are sold both in standalone branded shops, and as a part of a mix with other brands in local shoe stores. Standalones generally provide wider choice of models and sizes; local stores can help if you need to hunt for a specific model and size.

For, Private national fashion chain featuring many premium brands. Main location is Bilbao; some stores in San Sebastian and Zaragoza.

Eat

The Spanish are very passionate about their food and wine and Spanish cuisine. Spanish food can be described as quite light with a lot of vegetables and a huge variety of meat and fish. The Spanish cuisine does not use many spices; it relies only on the use of high quality ingredients to give a good taste. There are usually a variety of restaurants in most cities (Italian, Chinese, American fast food) if you would like to experience a variety of flavors.

Breakfast, Lunch and Dinner times

Spaniards have a different eating timetable than many people are used to.

The key thing to remember for a traveler is:

Breakfast (el desayuno) for most Spaniards is light and consists of just coffee and perhaps a galleta (like a graham cracker) or magdalena (sweet muffin-like bread). Later, some will go to a cafe for a pastry midmorning, but not too close to lunchtime.

"El aperitivo" is a light snack eaten around 12:00. However, this could include a couple of glasses of beer and a large filled baguette or a "pincho de tortilla".

Lunch (la comida) starts at 13:30-14:30 (though often not until 15:00) and was once typically followed by a short siesta, usually at summer when temperatures can be quite hot in the afternoon. This is the main meal of the day with two courses (el primer plato and el segundo plato followed by dessert. La comida and siesta are usually over by 17:00 at the latest. However, since life has become busier, there is no opportunity for a siesta.

Dinner (la cena) starts at 20:30 or 21, with most clientèle coming after 21. It is a lighter meal than lunch. In Madrid restaurants rarely open before 21:00 and most customers do not appear before 22:00.

There is also an afternoon snack that some take between la comida and la cena called la merienda. It is similar to a tea time and is taken around 18 or so.

Between the lunch and dinner times, most restaurants and cafes are closed, and it takes extra effort to find a place to eat if you missed lunch time. Despite this, you can always look for a bar and ask for a bocadillo, a baguette sandwich. There are bocadillos fríos, cold sandwiches, which can be filled with ham, cheese or any kind of embutido, and bocadillos calientes, hot sandwiches, filled with pork loin, tortilla, bacon, sausage and similar options with cheese. This can be a really cheap and tasty option if you find a good place.

Normally, restaurants in big cities don't close until midnight during the week and 2-3AM during the weekend.

Breakfast

Breakfast is eaten by most Spaniards. Traditional Spanish breakfast includes coffee or orange juice, and pastries or a small sandwich. In Madrid, it is also common to have hot chocolate with "churros" or "porras". In cafes, you can expect varieties of tortilla de patatas (see the Spanish dishes section), sometimes tapas (either breakfast variety or same kind as served in the evenings with alcohol).

Tapas

The entry level to Spanish food is found in bars as tapas, which are a bit like "starters" or "appetizers", but are instead considered side orders to accompany your drink. Some bars will offer a wide variety of different tapas; others specialize on a specific kind (like seafood-based). A Spanish custom is to have one tapa and one small drink at a bar, then go to the next bar and do the same. A group of two or more individuals may order two or more tapas or order raciones instead, which are a bit larger in order to share.

Pintxos

Pintxos (pronounced as pinchos) are unique to the Basque Region, and are similar to tapas, in that they are small portions typically served at bars, but with different styles, and traditions, and should not be referred to as tapas. Pintxos are traditionally finger food served on a sliced baguette, or on a wooden skewer, but it's not uncommon to find bars that have dispensed with that tradition, especially for higher end pintxos. Most pintxo bars will have a selection of pintxos to choose from on the bar itself, and some will have an additional menu posted you can order hot made to order pintxos from. In regions known for their pintxos, like San Sebastian, it's not uncommon to find very high end, and well prepared pintxos that would be at home on some of the worlds best restaurant menu's. Pintxo Prices are typically relatively inexpensive, and range from €1 - €5, and are usually ordered with a drink (for example: Txakoli, a dry wine, or Kalimotxo, red wine mixed with cola, both common in Basque Region) for an additional €1 - €3.

Fast food

Fast food has not yet established a strong grip on the Spaniards and you will find McDonalds and Burger King only in bigger towns in the usual places. The menu can be a surprise since it has been customized to appeal to the locals and beer, salads, yogurt (primarily Danone), and wine are prominent. Pizza is increasingly popular and you will find some outlets in bigger towns but it can be their own homegrown franchises, such as TelePizza. In spite of beer and wine on the menu, fast food is often seen as "kiddie food." American franchises generally charge higher Prices than in the United States, and fast food is not necessarily the cheapest alternative for eating out.

Restaurants

Seafood: on a seacoast, fresh seafood is widely available and quite affordable. In the inner regions, frozen (and poor quality) seafood can be frequently encountered outside few highly reputed (and expensive) restaurants. In coastal areas seafood deserves some attention, especially on the north Atlantic coast.

Quality seafood in Spain comes from Spain's northwestern region of Galicia. So restaurants with the words Gallego (Galician) will generally specialize in seafood. If you are feeling adventurous, you might want to try the Galician regional specialty Pulpo a la Gallega, which is boiled octopus served with paprika, rock salt and olive oil. Another adventurous option is Sepia which is cuttlefish, a relative of squid, or the various forms of Calamares (squid) that you can find in most seafood restaurants. If that isn't your style you can always order Gambas Ajillo (garlic shrimp), Pescado Frito (fried fish), Buñuelos de Bacalao (breaded and deep fried cod) or the ever-present Paella dishes.

Meat products are usually of very good quality, because Spain has maintained quite a high percentage of free range animals.

Ordering beef steaks is highly recommended, since most comes from free range cows from the mountains north of the city.

The presa ibérica, being "Iberico black pig shoulder blade cooked medium-rare and served with pea purée"

Pork cuts which are also highly coveted are those known as Presa Iberica and Secreto Iberico, an absolute must if found in the menu of any restaurant.

Soups: choice of soups beyond gazpacho is very limited in Spanish restaurants.

Water is frequently served without a specific request, and is normally charged for--unless it's included in your menu del dia. If you would like free tap water instead of bottled water, request "agua del grifo" (water from the tap). However, not all restaurants will offer this and you may be forced to order bottled water.

Appetizers such as bread, cheese, and other items may be brought to your table even if you didn't order them. You will be charged for them. If you do not want these appetizers, politely inform the waiter that you do not want them.

Tipping is not observed in Spain so don't tip (unless there was something absolutely exceptional about the service). As a result, people from countries where tipping is the norm (primarily the US) may find that waiters are not as attentive or courteous since they don't work for tips. This is less true in major resorts and cities where tipping is common. Look around at other diners to assess if tipping is appropriate.

World-level restaurants: There are several restaurants in Spain which are destinations in itself, becoming a sole reason to travel to a specific city. One of them is El Bulli in Roses.

Tipping and VAT

Service charges are included in the bill. You are free to tip if you are very pleased: you would typically leave the small change after paying with a note. Maybe at the most touristy places they expect you to give some extra, but Spanish people do not commonly do it.

VAT is-not-included is a common trick for mid-range and splurge restaurants: always check in menu whether VAT (10%, IVA in Spanish) is included in menu Prices.

Menú del día

Many restaurants offer a complete lunch meal for a fixed Price – "menú del día" – and this often works out as a bargain. Water or wine is commonly included in the Price.

Food & Wine Tours

Those looking for some orientation to the rich and diverse culinary traditions of Spain can consider going on a food tour. Options are plentiful in every city, and especially in Barcelona, San Sebastian, and Madrid. A quick Google search will reveal the most popular ones.

Touristy places

Typical Spanish food can be found all over the country, however top tourist destinations such as Costa Brava and Costa del Sol have turned all existing traditions upside down. Meaning that drinks are generally more expensive (about double) and quality is at its lowest. It is difficult to find proper Spanish food in the tourist centers.

Instead, you will get Schnitzel, original English breakfast, Pizza, Donner, and frozen fish. However, if you are prepared to look a little harder, then even in the busiest tourist towns, you can find some exceptional traditional Spanish restaurants. If you are on the coast then think fish and seafood and you won't be disappointed.

Non-Spanish cuisine

In most cities you can also find international cuisine such as Italian, Chinese, French, Thai, Japanese, Middle Eastern, Vietnamese, Argentinian, etc. The bigger the city, the more variety you can find.

For the past decade there has been a surge in the number of Irish pubs and Japanese restaurants to be found in most cities.

Specialties to buy

Cheese: Spain offers a wide variety of regional cheeses. Queso Manchego is the most famous one. Cabrales, Tetilla, Mahon are also popular.

Chorizo: Spain's most popular sausage is spiced cured, made from pork, ham, salt, garlic and pepper and is produced in multitude of varieties, in different sizes, shapes, short and long, spicy, in all different shades of red, soft, air dried and hard or smoked. Frequently contains emulgators and conservatives, so check ingredients if you feel sensitive.

Jamón (air dried ham): Jamón Serrano (Serrano ham): Is obtained from the salt meat of the back legs of the pig and air dried. This same product is given the name of trowel or paletilla when it is obtained from the front legs. Also it receives the names of jamón Iberico (Iberian) and jamón of bellota (acorn). They are specially famous jamones that takes place in Huelva (Spain), in Guijuelo (province Salamanca), in the Pedroches (province Cordova) and in Trevélez (province of Granada). Jamón Iberico is made from free range pigs.

Judging by Boqueria in Barcelona, Jamon Iberico starts at €80/kg, and Jamon Serrano is about €25/kg. One well known chain in Spain is

Mesón Cinco Jotas, which is known by locals for their expensive, but good quality ham.

Visiting Spain without trying Jamon Iberico would be considered a crime by most Spaniards. Spaniards treat their ham very seriously and types and qualities of ham vary in a similar way to wine. Quality ham is generally expensive but has little to do with the many cheaper versions available. The diet of the pig is the most important factor in determining the quality of the ham. The least expensive ham comes from pigs fed on normal grains whereas medium grade pigs are raised on a combination of acorns and grains. The top tier pigs are fed exclusively on acorns and their hams are not considered to be the best grade without an "acorn fed" stamp. These top grade hams have a rich flavor and an oily texture but to non-connoisseurs, glossiness and the presence of white lines of fat crisscrossing a slice of ham is generally a good indicator of its quality.

Morcilla: Black sausages made from pig blood, generally made with rice or onion. Sometimes flavoured with anise, it comes as a fresh, smoked or air dried variety.

Spanish dishes

Typical Spanish dishes include:

Aceitunas, Olivas: Olives, often served for nibbling.

Bocadillo de Calamares: Fried battered calamari served in a ciabatta sandwich with lemon juice.

Boquerones en vinagre: Anchovies marinated in vinegar with garlic and parsley.

Caracoles: Snails in a hot sauce.

Calamares en su tinta: Squid in its ink.

Chipirones a la plancha: Grilled little squids.

Churros: A fried horn-shaped snack, sometimes referred to as a Spanish doughnut. Typical for a Spanish breakfast or for tea time. Served with hot chocolate drink.

Empanadas Gallegas: Meat or tuna pies are also very popular in Madrid. Originally from region of Galicia.

Ensaladilla Rusa (Russian Salad): This potato salad dish of Russian origin, widely consumed in parts of Eastern Europe and the Middle East, is strangely enough, extremely popular in Spain.

Fabada asturiana: Bean stew from Asturias.

Gambas al ajillo: Prawns with garlic and chili. Fantastic hot stuff.

Gazpacho Andaluz: Cold vegetable soup. Best during the hot weather. It's like drinking a salad.

Lentejas: A dish made from lentils with chorizo sausage and/or Serrano ham.

Mariscos: Shellfish from the province of Pontevedra.

Merluza a la Vizcaina: The Spanish are not very fond of sauces. One of the few exceptions is merluza a la Vasca. The dish contains hake (fish of the cod family) prepared with white asparagus and green peas.

Potajes or pucheros: Garbanzo beans stew at its best

Paella or Paella Valenciana: This is a rice dish originally from Valencia. Rice is grown locally in what look like wheat fields, and this is the variety used in paella. The original paella used chicken and rabbit, and saffron (el azafran). Nowadays varieties of paella can be found all over Spain, many containing seafood. Locals suggest to find true paella in large parties like a wedding in a village, but few restaurants still can compete with it.

Patatas Bravas: Fried potatoes which have been previously boiled, served with a patented spicy sauce. They are potatoes cut in form of dices or prism, of one to two centimeters of size approximately and that they are fried in oil and accompanied by a sharp sauce that spills on potatoes using hot spices.

Pescaíto frito: Delicious fried fish that can be found mainly in southern Spain

Pimientos rellenos: Peppers stuffed with minced meat or seafood. The peppers in Spain taste different than all other peppers in Europe.

Potaje de espinacas y garbanzos: Chick pea stew with spinach. Typical of Seville.

Revuelto de ajetes con setas: Scrambled eggs with fresh garlic sprouts and wild mushrooms. Also commonly contains shrimps.

Setas al ajillo/Gambas al ajillo: Shrimps or wild mushrooms fried in garlic.

Sepia con alioli: Fried cuttlefish with garlic mayonnaise. Very popular among tourists.

Tortilla de patatas: Spanish egg omelet with fried potato. Probably the most popular dish in Spain. You can easily assess how good a restaurant is by having a small piece of its potato tortillas. Frequently it is made also with onion, depending on the zone or the pleasure. The potatoes must be fried in oil (preferably of olive), and they are left soaking with the scrambled egg for more than 10 minutes, although better if it is average hour so that they are soaked and they acquire the suitable consistency.

Drink

Tea and Coffee

Spanish people are very passionate about the quality, intensity and taste of their coffee and good freshly brewed coffee is available almost everywhere.

The usual choices are solo, the milk-less espresso version; cortado, solo with a dash of milk; con leche, solo with milk added; and manchado, coffee with lots of milk (sort of like the French cafe au lait). Asking for caffee latte will likely result in less milk than you are used to--it's always OK to ask for adding extra milk.

Regional variants can be found, such as bombón in Eastern Spain, solo with condensed milk.

Starbucks is the only national chain operating in Spain. Locals argue that it cannot compete with small local cafes in quality of coffee and it's frequented mostly by tourists, thought it has become somewhat popular with young "hip" people. It is not present in smaller cities but it's basically everywhere in Barcelona or Madrid.

Café de Jamaica offers many kinds of coffee as well as infusions.

Bracafe that means 'brasilian coffee' offers high quality coffee.

If you eat for €20 per dinner, you will never be served a good tea; expect Pompadour or Lipton. It takes some effort to find a good tea if you spend most time of the day in touristy places.

Alcohol

The drinking/purchasing age of alcoholic beverages in Spain is 18. People under this age are forbidden to drink and buy alcoholic drinks, although enforcement in tourist and clubbing areas is lax. Drinking in the streets has recently been banned (although it is still a common practice in most nightlife areas). Alcohol may not available in some stores between 10 p.m. and 9 a.m. without the store possessing a specific license to sell alcohol.

Try an absinthe cocktail (the fabled liquor was never outlawed here, but it is not a popular drink in Spain).

Bars

Probably one of the best places to meet people in Spain is in bars. Everyone visits them and they are always busy and sometimes bursting with people. There is no age restriction imposed to enter these premises. but children and teenagers often will not be served alcoholic drinks. Age restrictions for the consumption of alcohol are clearly posted at bars but are enforced only intermittently. It is common to see an entire family at a bar.

It's important to know the difference between a pub (which closes at 3-3:30 a.m.) and a club (which opens until 6-8 a.m. but is usually deserted early in the night).

On weekends, the time to go out for copas (drinks) usually starts at about 11 p.m.-1 a.m. which is somewhat later than in North and Central Europe. Before that, people usually do any number of things, have some tapas (raciones, algo para picar), eat a "real" dinner in a restaurant, stay at home with family, or go to cultural events. If you want to go dancing, you will find that most of the clubs in Madrid are relatively empty before midnight (some do not even open until 1 a.m.) and most won't get crowded until 3 a.m. People usually go to pubs, then go to the clubs until 6-8 a.m.

For a true Spanish experience, after a night of dancing and drinking it is common to have a breakfast of chocolate con churros with your friends before going home. (CcC is a small cup of thick, melted chocolate served with freshly fried sweet fritters used for dipping in the chocolate and should be tried, if only for the great taste.)

Bars are mainly to have drink and a small tapa while socializing and decompressing from work or studies. Usually Spaniards can control their alcohol consumption better than their northern European neighbors and drunken people are rarely seen at bars or on the streets. A drink, if ordered without an accompanying tapa, is often served with a "minor" or inexpensive tapa as a courtesy.

Size and Price of tapas changes a lot throughout Spain. For instance, it's almost impossible to get free tapas in big cities like Valencia or Barcelona, excluding Madrid where there are several Tapa Bars althought some times are a bit expensive. You can eat for free (just paying for the drinks), with huge tapas and cheap Prices at cities like Granada, Badajoz or Salamanca.

The tapa, and the related pincho, trace their existence in Spain to both acting as a cover ("Tapa") on top of a cup of wine to prevent flies from accessing it, and as a requirement of law when serving wine at an establishment during the middle ages.

Beer

The Spanish beer is not too bad and well worth a try. Most popular local brands include San Miguel, Cruzcampo, Mahou, Estrella Damm, Ámbar, Estrella de Galicia, Moritz, Keller and many others, including local brands at most cities; import beers are also available. A great beer is 'Mezquita' (Cervezas Alhambra), try to find it! Also "Legado de Yuste" is one of the best beer made in Spain, and is quite extended, but more expensive than a normal 'caña'. Most brands offer non-alcoholic beer.

In Spain, beer is often served from a tap in 25 cl ("caña") or 33 cl ("tubo") tube glasses. Bigger servings are rare, but you can also ask for a "corto", "zurito" (round the Basque country) or simply "una cerveza" or "tanque" (south of the country) to get a half size beer, perfect to drink in one go and get quickly to the next bar while having tapas.

If you're in Zaragoza (or Aragon, in general), the Pilsner-type Ambar (5.2% alc.) and the stronger Export (double malt, 7.0% alc.) are available. Ambar 1900: Its production began in 1996. The system of fermentation to room temperature is used. Marlen is a beer of traditional manufacture using malted barley and hops.

While beer production has been dominated by big brands, nowadays a new brew appears in the market quite regularly. To date there are around 400 producers of craft beer in Spain, although it represents just a tiny fraction (0.3 percent) of the country beer market, brews are growing like beer-foam. Between 2008 and 2015 it grew 1.600%. The [barcelonaeatlocal.com/hottest-craft-beers-in-spain/ Spanish Craft Beer revolution] is challenging big brands.

Particularly on hot summer days people will drink a refreshing "clara" which is a light beer mixed with lemon/lemonade.

Cava

Cava is Spanish sparkling wine and the name went from Spanish Champagne to Cava was after a long lasting dispute with the French. The Spanish called it for a long time champan, but the French argued that champagne can be made only from grapes grown in the Champagne region in France. Nevertheless, Cava is a quite successful sparkling wine and 99% of the production comes from the area around Barcelona.

Cider (Sidra)

@ciderexplorer

Can be found in the Galicia, Asturias, Cantabria and Pais Vasco. This is slightly different to ciders found elsewhere in the world, since it not carbonated. It is often served in small doses (culines) that are poured from great height (called escanciar) in order to give it the feel of a carbonated beverage. This practice is particularly common in Asturias, although nowadays many establishments provide a small machine that makes the slightly difficult process of escanciar easy to do at your table.

Horchata

A milky non-alcoholic drink made of tigernuts and sugar. Alboraia, a small town close to Valencia, is regarded as a best place where horchata is produced.

Sangria

Sangria is drink made of wine and fruits and usually is made from simple wines. You will find sangria in areas frequented by tourists. Spanish prepare sangria for fiestas and hot summer, and not every day as seen in touristic regions like Mallorca.

Sangria in restaurants aimed for foreigners are best avoided, but it is a very good drink to try if a Spaniard prepares it for a fiesta!

Sherry (Fino)

The pale sherry wine around Jerez called "fino" is fortified with alcohol to 15 percent. If you would like to have one in a bar you have to order a fino. Manzanilla is bit salty, good as an appetizer. Amontillado and Oloroso are a different types of sherry were the oxidative aging process has taken the lead.

Wine

Spain is a country with great wine-making and drinking traditions: 22% of Europe's wine growing area is in Spain, however the production is about half of what the French produce.

Regions: most famous wines come from Rioja region, less known but also important come from Ribera del Duero, Priorato, Toro and Jumilla . The latter are becoming more and more popular and are slightly less expensive than Rioja wines. White, rose and red wines are produced, but the red wines are certainly the most important ones.

Grapes: main red grapes are Tempranillo, Garnacha, Monastrell and Mencia. Primary white grape used is Albarino, and the grapes used in Jerez are: 'Pedro Ximenez and Palomino.

Specific names: Valdepenas is good value for money. Whites: Belondrade Y Lurton is regarded as greatest white wine in Spain. Vina Sol is good as a mass product, with fruity taste.

Grades: Spanish quality wines are produced using an aging process and they have been in a oak barrel for at least one year before they can be labeled Crianza and then spend another two years in a bottle before been sold. Reservas are aged for five years and Gran Reservas are aged for 10 years.

Prices: Spain has seen a tremendous rise in wine Prices over the last decade and Spanish wines are not as much of a bargain as they used to be. However you will still find 5, 10 and 20 year old wines at affordable Prices especially when compared with similar quality wines from Australia, Chile, France, and the US.

Wine bars: they are more and more popular. In short, a wine bar is a sophisticated tapas bar where you can order wine by the glass. You will immediately see a blackboard with the wines that are available and the Price per glass.

In a bar: for red wine in a bar, ask "un tinto por favor", for white wine "un blanco por favor", for rose: "un rosado por favor". In certain bars you have to specify "un crianza" (for an aged wine) or "un Rioja, un Ribera" (for a wine from Rioja or Ribera de Duero) if you don't want a cheap wine.

Wine tourism: Spain´s wine regions offer many opportunities to enjoy wine tasting at wineries and local food. Most popular wine destinations are Rioja due to its tradition as a red wine producing region, Jerez de la Frontera, due to its proximity to holiday destination and the impressive wineries that specialise in Sherry production and the wine region south of Barcelona in Penedes. Many interesting itineraries and routes are proposed by local wine organisations. List of wine tourism routes in Spain

Wine-based drinks: young people in Spain have developed their own way to have wine. When having botellones (big outdoor parties with drink and lots of people), most of them mix some red wine with Coke and drink it straight from the Coke bottle. The name of this drink is calimocho or kalimotxo (in the Basque Country and Navarre) and is really very popular... But don't ask for it while in an upper class bar or among adults, since they will most certainly not approve of the idea! As a general rule, any wine that comes in a glass bottle is considered "too good" to make kalimotxo.

Accommodation

There are three names for hotel-like accommodation in large cities in Spain: hotel, hostal and pension. It is important not to confuse a hostel with a hostal; a hostel offers backpacker-type accommodation with shared rooms, whereas a hostal is very similar to a guest house and is generally cheaper than a hotel.

There are many types of tourist accommodation, ranging from hotels, pensions and rented villas, to camping and even monasteries.

"10% VAT is not included" is a common trick for mid-range guesthouses and hotels: always check the small print when you choose your place to stay. VAT is IVA in Spanish.

Small villages

Besides the coasts, Spain is rich in small tourist-friendly inland villages, like Alquezar: with narrow medieval streets, charming silence and isolation, still good selection of affordable restaurants and accommodation.

Casa rural, the bed and breakfasts of Spain

For a more homely sort of accommodation consider the casa rural. A casa rural is the rough equivalent to a bed and breakfast or a gîte. Not all houses are situated in the countryside, as the name implies. Some are situated in the smaller towns, and they are in virtually every province.

Casas rurales vary in quality and Price throughout Spain. They are strictly controlled and inspected.

Hotels

Many foreign visitors stay in hotels that have been organised by tour operators who offer package holidays to the popular resorts on the costas and islands. However, for the independent traveller, there are hotels all over the country in all categories and to suit every budget. In fact, due to the well developed internal and foreign tourism markets Spain may well be one of the best served European countries in terms of numbers and quality of hotels. Spain also includes some of the most luxurious hotels in Europe (Spain In Style) which are more towards the higher Price range for hotels.

Paradores

A parador (inn) is a state-owned hotel in Spain (rating from 3 to 5 stars). These are a chain of hotels founded in 1928 by the Spanish King Alfonso XIII. The unique aspects of paradores are their location and their history. Found mostly in historical buildings, such as convents, Moorish castles (like La Alhambra), or haciendas, paradores are the exact opposite of the uncontrolled development found in coastal regions like the Costa del Sol. Hospitality has been harmoniously integrated with the restoration of castles, palaces and convents, rescuing from ruin and abandonment monuments representative of Spain's historical and cultural heritage.

For example the parador in Santiago de Compostela is located next to the Cathedral in a former royal hospital built in the year 1499. Rooms are decorated in an old-fashioned way, but nevertheless have modern facilities. Other notable paradores are in Arcos de la Frontera, Ronda, Santillana del Mar (Altamira cave) as well as more than 100 other destination all over Spain.

Paradores serve breakfast (about €10) and often have very good local cuisine typical of their region (about €25).

Accommodation Prices are good value, when you consider that the hotels are often found in the heart of scenic areas, varying from €85 for a double room to €245 for a twin room (like in Granada). Two of the most beautiful paradors are in Léon and Santiago de Compostela.

There are some promotions available:

Over 60 year olds can enjoy a discount.

Youngsters under 30 can visit the paradors at a 10% discount. The discount also applies to companions over 30.

Two nights half board have a discount of 20%.

A dreamweek of 6 nights is cheaper.

5 nights at €42 per person.

The promotions do not always apply, especially in August they are not valid, and may require advance bookings.

Hostels

There are plenty of hostels, mostly in Madrid. Prices vary from €15 to €25 per night.

Xanascat is the National Network of Youth Hostels of Catalonia if you are visiting Barcelona, Girona, Taragona or other locations in the region.

Apartment rental

Short-term, self-catering apartment rental is an option for travellers who want to stay in one place for a week or more. Accommodations range from small apartments to villas.

The number of holiday rentals available depends on the area of Spain you are planning to visit. Although they are common in coastal areas, big capitals and other popular tourist cities, if you plan to visit small inland towns, you will find casas rurales more easily.

Camping

Camping is the least expensive lodging option.

Stay safe

Police

There are four kinds of police:

'Policía Municipal' or 'Local' (metropolitan police), In Barcelona: Guardia Urbana. Uniforms change from town to town, but they use to wear black or blue clothes with pale blue shirt and a blue cap (or white helmet) with a checkered white-and-blue strip. This kind of police keeps order and rules the traffic inside cities, and they are the best people in case you are lost and need some directions. Although you can't officially report theft to them, they will escort you to 'Policia Nacional' headquarters if required, and they will escort the suspects to be arrested also, if needed.

'Policía Nacional' wear dark blue clothes and blue cap (sometimes replaced by a baseball-like cap), unlike Policía Municipal, they do not have a checkered flag around their cap/helmet. Inside cities, all offenses/crimes should be reported to them, although the other police corps would help anyone who needs to report an offense.

'Guardia Civil' keeps the order outside cities, in the country, and regulates traffic in the roads between cities. You would probably see them guarding official buildings, or patrolling the roads. They wear plain green military-like clothes; some of them wear a strange black helmet ('tricornio') resembling a toreador cap, but most of them use green caps or white motorcycle helmets.

Given that Spain has a high grade of political autonomy released to its regional governments, four of them have created regional law forces: the Policía Foral in Navarre, the Ertzaintza in the Basque Country or the Mossos d'Esquadra in Catalonia. These forces have the almost the same competences as the Policía Nacional in their respective territories.

All kinds of police also wear high-visibility clothing ("reflective" jackets) while directing traffic, or in the road.

Theft

Spain is a safe country, but you should take some basic precautions encouraged in the entire world:

Thieves prefer stealth to direct confrontation so it is unlikely that you will be hurt in the process, but exercise caution all the same.

There have been instances where thieves on motorbikes drive by women and grab their purses, so keep a tight hold on yours even if you don't see anyone around.

Try not to show the money you have in your wallet or purse.

Always watch your bag or purse in touristic places, buses, trains and meetings. A voice message reminding that is played in most of the bus/train stations and airports.

Do not carry large amounts of money with you, unless needed. Use your credit card (Spain is the first country in number of cash points and most shops/restaurants accept it). Of course, use it with caution.

Beware of pickpockets when visiting areas with large numbers of people, like crowded buses or the Puerta del Sol(in Madrid). If you report a thief, people are generally helpful.

Don't hesitate to report crimes to local police.

In general, you must bear in mind that those areas with a larger number of foreign visitors, like some crowded vacation resorts in the East Coast, are much more likely to attract thieves than places which are not so popular among tourists.

Avoid gypsy women offering rosemary, refuse it always; they will read your future, ask for some money, and your pocket will probably be picked. Some gypsy women will also approach you on the street repeating "Buena suerte" ("good luck") as a distraction for another gypsy woman to try to pickpocket you. Avoid them at all costs.

A great tourist attraction is the Flea Market (el Rastro) in Madrid on the weekends. However, as it is nearly standing room only - it is also an attraction for pickpockets. They operate in groups... be extremely cautious in these tight market type environments as it is very common to be targeted... especially if you stand out as a tourist or someone with money. Try to blend in and not stand out and you will likely not be at as much risk.

Women who carry purses should always put the straps across their bodies. Always hold on to the purse itself and keep it in front of your body. Keep one hand on the bottom, as pickpockets can otherwise slit the bottom without you ever knowing.

Never place anything on the back of a chair or on the floor next to you, keep it on your person always.

If you must use an ATM, do not flash the money you have just picked up.

Scams

Some people could try to take advantage of your ignorance of local customs.

In Spanish cities, all taxis should have a visible fare table. Do not agree a fixed Price to go from an airport to a city: in most cases, the taxi driver will be earning more money than without a preagreed tariff. Many taxi drivers will also demand a tip from foreign customers or even from national ones on the way to and from the airport. You might round up to the nearest euro when paying though.

In many places of Madrid, especially near Atocha station, and also in the Ramblas of Barcelona, there are people ('trileros') who play the "shell game". They will "fish" you if you play, and they will most likely pick your pocket if you stop to see other people play.

Before paying the bill in bars and restaurants, always check the bill and carefully scrutinize it. Some staff will often attempt to squeeze a few extra euros out of unsuspecting tourists by charging for things they did not eat or drink, or simply overcharging. This is true in both touristy and non-touristy areas. If you feel overcharged, bring it to their attention and/or ask to see a menu. It is also sometimes written (in English only) at the bottom of a bill that a tip is not included: remember that tipping is optional in Spain and Spanish people commonly leave loose change only and no more than a 5%-8% of the Price of what they have consumed (not an American-style 15-20%), so avoid being fooled into leaving more than you have to.

Other things you should know

Spanish cities can be LOUD at night, especially on weekends.

All stores, hotels and restaurants should have an official complaint form, in case you need it.

The emergency telephone number (police, firefighters, ambulances) is 112. You may call it from any phone at no cost, in case you need to.

Drugs

In Spain possession and consumption of illegal drugs at private places is not prosecuted. Taking drugs in public and possession, for personal use, will be fined from €300 to €3000 depending of the drug and the quantity that you carry on, you will not get arrested unless you have large quantities destined for street sale.

Stay healthy

Pharmaceuticals are not sold at supermarkets, only at 'farmacias' (pharmacies), identified with a green cross or a Hygeia's cup. Nearly every city and town has at least one 24 hour pharmacy; for those that close at night, the law requires a poster with the address of the nearest pharmacy, possibly in one of the nearby streets or towns.

People from the European Union and a few more European countries can freely use the public health system, if they have the appropriate intereuropean sanitary card. That card does not work in private hospitals. Agreements are established to treat people from a few American countries; see the Tourspain link below for more info.

However, do not hesitate to go to any healthcare facility should you be injured or seriously ill, as it would be illegal for them not to treat you, even if you are uninsured.

Though most foreigners tend to think Spain is a warm place, it can be terribly cold in winter, especially in the Central Region and in the North, and in some places it is also rainy in summer. Remember to travel with adequate clothes.

In summer, avoid direct exposure to sunlight for long periods of time to prevent sunburn and heatstroke. Drink water, walk on the shady side of street and keep a container of sun cream (suntan lotion) handy.

Most cities have a good water supply, especially Madrid, but you may prefer bottled water to the alkaline taste of water in the east and south.

Smoking

On 21 December 2010, the Spanish Parliament approved a law prohibiting smoking in all indoor public and work places and near hospitals and in playgrounds, becoming effective on 2 January 2011. Smoking is now banned in all enclosed public spaces and places of work, in public transportation, and in outdoor public places near hospitals and in playgrounds. Smoking is also banned in outdoor sections of bars and restaurants. Smoking is banned in television broadcasts as well.

Respect

Culture and identity

Spaniards in general are very patriotic about both their country and the region in which they live. Avoid arguments about whether or not people from Catalonia, Galicia or the Basque Country are Spaniards. Safety is generally not a concern in case you engage in an argument, but you will be dragged in a long, pointless discussion.

Spaniards are generally very interested in maintaining their linguistic and cultural connections with Latin America. However, most Spaniards are also quick to point out they are Europeans and do not understand the common North American notion that "Hispanics," including Spaniards, are somehow all the same. People from other Spanish-speaking countries or backgrounds may encounter a variety of receptions from being embraced as cultural kin to rejection or apathy.

Spaniards are not as religious as the media sometimes presents them, but they are and always were a mostly Catholic country (73% officially, although just 10% admit practicing and just a 20% admit being believers); respect this and avoid making any comments that could offend. In particular, religious festivals, Holy Week (Easter), and Christmas are very important to Spaniards. Tolerance to all religions should be observed, especially in large urban areas like Madrid, Barcelona, Valencia, Seville or Malaga (where people and temples of all beliefs can be found) or different regions in southern Spain, which may have a sizeable Muslim population (which accounts for almost a 4,5% of the country's total).

Despite being a Catholic majority country, homosexuality is tolerated in Spain and public display of same-sex affection would not stir hostility a majority of the time. In fact, same-sex marriages are legal and recognized by the government and provide legal benefits to same-sex couples. However, a gay friendly country does not always necessarily mean that the Spaniards are friendly to gays: (people in places like Madrid or Barcelona, which are 2 of the largest urban areas in Europe, will obviously have a more open view than those from rural areas). As in any other place, elderly people do usually have far more conservative points of view. Still, violence against gays is rarely heard of and Spain should be safe for most gay and lesbian travelers.

Avoid talking about the former colonial past and especially about the "Black Legend." Regardless of what you may have heard Spain had several ministers and military leaders of mixed race serving in the military during the colonial era and even a Prime Minister born in the Philippines (Marcelo Azcarraga Palmero). Many Spaniards take pride in their history and former imperial glories. People from Spain's former colonies (Latin America, Equatorial Guinea, the Philippines, Western Sahara and Northern Morocco) make up a majority of foreign immigrants in Spain (a 58%) along with the Chinese, Africans and Eastern Europeans. Equally, Spain is one of the main investors and economic and humanitarian aid donors to Latin America and Africa.

Bullfighting is seen by many Spaniards as a cultural heritage icon, but the disaffection with bullfighting is increasing in all big cities and obviously among animal activist groups within the country. Many urban Spaniards would consider bullfighting a show aimed at foreign tourists and elder people from the countryside, and some young Spaniards will feel offended if their country is associated with it. To illustrate how divided the country is, many Spaniards point to the royal family: King Juan Carlos and his daughter are avid fans, while his wife and the Heir Prince do not care for the sport. Bullfights and related events, such as the annual San Fermin Pamplona bull-runs, make up a multimillion-dollar industry and draw many tourists, both foreign and Spaniard. In addition, bullfighting was recently banned in the northeastern region of Catalonia and has also been outlawed in several towns and counties all over the country.

Avoid mentioning the past, such as the former fascist dictatorship of Francisco Franco, who ruled Spain from 1939 to 1975, and especially the Civil War of 1936-1939. Many symbols, pictures, statues and monuments affiliated with the Franco regime have been outlawed and possible fines and jail time could result if you violate these laws. This was a painful past as Franco ruled Spain with an iron fist, executing many Spaniards who violated the anti-democratic laws of the regime. Nonetheless, one of the best periods of economic growth in Spain was the one that took place during the last years of Franco's regime, so some older Spaniards may have supportive views of Franco's ultranationalist and anticommunist ideology, so talking against Franco in front of them may be considered offensive.

Socializing

It is customary to kiss friends, family, and acquaintances on both cheeks upon seeing each other and saying goodbye. Male-to-male kisses of this sort are limited to family members or to very close friends; otherwise a firm handshake is expected instead (same as in France or Italy). A happy medium is the traditional abrazo (hug) which is usually done to people that you haven't seen in a long time and/or are very glad to see, regardless of gender (male-to-male is somewhat more common). When somebody expects a hug he/she usually will throw his/her arms towards you: this is more common than you may think, but don't do it with complete strangers as it's probably a ruse to get your wallet.

Related to this, Spaniards are keen to maintain physical contact while talking, such as putting a hand on your shoulder, patting your back, etc. These should be taken as signs of friendship done among relatives, close friends and colleagues.

When in a car, the elderly and pregnant always ride in the passenger's seat, unless they request not to.

While Spaniards may not always be the most punctual people in the world, you should never arrive late to appointments; this will seem very bad to most people.

If you are staying at a Spaniard's home, bring shoes to wear inside such as slippers. Walking around barefoot in the house is viewed as unsanitary and also an easy way to catch a cold.

In Spanish beaches it is okay for women to sunbathe topless. This practice is particularly common in tourist areas. Full nudity is practised in "clothing-optional" or nudist beaches.

Eating and drinking

During lunch or dinner, Spaniards do not begin eating until everyone is seated and ready to eat. Likewise, they do not leave the table until everyone is finished eating. Table manners are otherwise standard and informal, although this also depends on the place you are eating. When the bill comes, it is common to pay equally, regardless of the amount or Price each has consumed.

When Spaniards receive a gift or are offered a drink or a meal, they usually refuse for a while, so as not to seem greedy. This sometimes sparks arguments among especially reluctant people, but it is seen as polite. Remember to offer more than once (on the third try, it must be fairly clear if they will accept it or not). On the other hand, if you are interested in the offer, politely smile and decline it, saying that you don't want to be a nuisance, etc., but relent and accept when they insist.

Spaniards rarely drink or eat in the street. Bars will rarely offer the option of food to take away but "tapas" are easily available. Especially unheard of until recently was the "doggy bag." However, in the last few years, taking leftovers home from a restaurant, although still not common, has become somewhat less of a stigma than it once was. One asks for "un taper" (derived from "Tupperware") or "una caja." Older Spaniards are still likely to frown on this.

Appearing drunk in public is generally frowned upon, though it's somewhat more accepted if you're a foreigner - but drunk rowdy foreigners are a negative stereotype in Spain so try to be respectful.

Cope

Among Spaniards, lunch time is usually between 13:00 and 14:30, while dinner time is around 21:00. However, in special celebrations, dinner can be as late as 22:00. Almost all businesses close between 14:30 and 17:00, so plan your shopping and sight-seeing accordingly. Shopping malls and supermarkets, however, are usually open from 9:30 to 22:00, and there are several 24 h shops, usually owned by Chinese immigrants.

Spanish cities can be noisy in some areas so be warned.

Contact

The main mobile network operators in Spain are Yoigo, Vodafone, Movistar and Orange. As in most of Europe voice and data coverage is generally good in urban areas, however it can be patchy in rural locations. OpenSignal provide a Spain cell coverage map allowing comparison between all the networks.

When using a laptop in an outdoor location, always be aware of your surroundings and the location of your belongings. Also be aware that even though it is not yet illegal to use unsecured wi-fi signals, there is work being done on the relevant laws and it may become illegal very soon.

"Locutorios" (Call Shops) are widely spread in bigger cities and touristy locations. In Madrid or Toledo it's very easy to find one. Making calls from "Locutorios" tend to be much cheaper, especially international calls (usually made through VoIP). They are usually a good pick for calling home.

Cheap mobile phones (less than €50) with some pre-paid minutes are sold at FNAC (Plaza Callao if you're staying in Madrid, or El Triangle if you're staying in Barcelona) or any phone operator's shop (Vodafone, Movistar, Orange) and can be purchased without many formalities (ID is usually required). Topping-up is then done by buying scratch cards from the small stores "Frutos Secos," supermarkets, vending points (often found in tobacco shops) or kiosks -- recharging via the internet or via an ATM does not work with foreign credit cards.

To call home cheap you may opt to buy prepaid calling cards which are widely available in newspapers or grocery stores around the city. Simply ask for a "tarjeta telefonica".

When travelling in Spain is not easy getting connected, Internet pre-paid cards can be purchased but with few formalities. Wi-Fi points in bars and cafeterias are available after ordering, and most Hotels offer Wi-Fi connection in common areas for their guests.

Prepaid portable WiFi Hot spot service is now available in Spain (provided by tripNETer and AlldayInternet) which allows the connection to any WiFi device: Smart-phones, Tablets, PCs…

You can rent a mobile Wi-Fi hotspot (4G/LTE) for short term period at a reasonable Price. Some companies such as My Webspot provide unlimited internet for the duration you need in Spain (from 5€ per day). It is delivered to your hotel or at the airport. A good solution to stay connected, and place international calls with your favorite AppsCreate category.

Experiences in Spain

Barcelona

Barcelona is an enchanting seaside city with boundless culture, fabled architecture and a world-class drinking and dining scene.

Architecture of the Ages

Barcelona's architectural treasures span 2000-plus years. Towering temple columns, ancient city walls and subterranean stone corridors provide a window into Roman-era Barcino. Fast forward a thousand years to the Middle Ages by taking a stroll through the shadowy lanes of the Gothic quarter, past tranquil plazas and soaring 14th-century cathedrals. In other parts of town bloom the sculptural masterpieces of Modernisme, a mix of ingenious and whimsical creations by Gaudí and his Catalan architectural contemporaries. Barcelona has also long inspired artists, including Salvador Dalí, Pablo Picasso and Joan Miró, whose works are in bold display in the city's myriad museums.

A Moveable Feast

The masters of molecular gastronomy – Albert Adrià, Carles Abellan et al – are part of the long and celebrated tradition of Catalan cooking. Simple, flavourful ingredients – seafood, jamón (cured ham), market-fresh produce – are transformed into remarkable delicacies and then served in captivating settings. Feast on hearty, rich paella at an outdoor table overlooking the sea or step back to the 1920s at an elegant art nouveau dining room. Barcelona's wide-ranging palate adds further complexity: Basque-style tapas bars, Galician seafood taverns, avant-garde Japanese restaurants and sinful chocolate shops are all essential parts of the culinary landscape.

Under the Iberian Sun

The deep blue Mediterranean beckons. Sun-drenched beaches make a fine backdrop to a jog, bike ride or long leisurely stroll along the seaside – followed by a refreshing dip. You can also enjoy the view from out on the water while kayaking, stand-up paddleboarding or taking it easy on a sunset cruise. Looming behind the city, the rolling forest-covered Collserola Hills provide a scenic setting for hiking, mountain biking or just admiring the view. Closer to the city centre, hilltop Montjuïc offers endless exploring amid botanic and sculpture gardens, an old castle and first-rate museums with panoramic views at every turn.

Twenty-four Hour Party People

The night holds limitless possibilities in Barcelona. Start with sunset drinks from a panoramic terrace or dig your heels in the sand at a rustic beachside chiringuito. As darkness falls, live music transforms the city: the rapid-fire rhythms of flamenco, brassy jazz spilling out of basements, and hands-in-the-air indie-rock at vintage concert halls. Towards midnight the bars fill. Take your pick from old-school taverns adorned with 19th-century murals, plush lounges in lamp-lit medieval chambers or boisterous cava bars. If you're still standing at 3am, hit the clubs and explore Barcelona's unabashed wild side.

Experiences in Barcelona

La Sagrada Família

Top choice church in La Sagrada Família & L'Eixample

Price - adult/concession/under 11yr €15/13/free

Hours - 9am-8pm Apr-Sep, to 6pm Oct-Mar

Contact - http://www.sagradafamilia.cat; 93 208 04 14

Location - Carrer de Mallorca 401, Barcelona, Spain

If you have time for only one sightseeing outing, this should be it. La Sagrada Família inspires awe by its sheer verticality, and in the manner of the medieval cathedrals it emulates, it's still under construction after more than 130 years. When completed, the highest tower will be more than half as high again as those that stand today.

Unfinished it may be, but it attracts around 2.8 million visitors a year and is the most visited monument in Spain. The most important recent tourist was Pope Benedict XVI, who consecrated the church in a huge ceremony in November 2010.

The Temple Expiatori de la Sagrada Família (Expiatory Temple of the Holy Family) was Antoni Gaudí's all-consuming obsession. Given the commission by a conservative society that wished to build a temple as atonement for the city's sins of modernity, Gaudí saw its completion as his holy mission. As funds dried up, he contributed his own, and in the last years of his life he was never shy of pleading with anyone he thought a likely donor.

Gaudí devised a temple 95m long and 60m wide, able to seat 13,000 people, with a central tower 170m high above the transept (representing Christ) and another 17 of 100m or more. The 12 along the three facades represent the Apostles, while the remaining five represent the Virgin Mary and the four evangelists. With his characteristic dislike for straight lines (there were none in nature, he said), Gaudí gave his towers swelling outlines inspired by the weird peaks of the holy mountain Montserrat outside Barcelona, and encrusted them with a tangle of sculpture that seems an outgrowth of the stone.

At Gaudí's death, only the crypt, the apse walls, one portal and one tower had been finished. Three more towers were added by 1930, completing the northeast (Nativity) facade. In 1936 anarchists burned and smashed the interior, including workshops, plans and models. Work began again in 1952, but controversy has always clouded progress. Opponents of the continuation of the project claim that the computer models based on what little of Gaudí's plans survived the anarchists' ire have led to the creation of a monster that has little to do with Gaudí's plans and style. It is a debate that appears to have little hope of resolution. Like or hate what is being done, the fascination it awakens is undeniable.

Guesses on when construction might be complete range from the 2020s to the 2040s. Even before reaching that point, some of the oldest parts of the church, especially the apse, have required restoration work.

Inside, work on roofing over the church was completed in 2010. The roof is held up by a forest of extraordinary angled pillars. As the pillars soar towards the ceiling, they sprout a web of supporting branches, creating the effect of a forest canopy. The tree image is in no way fortuitous – Gaudí envisaged such an effect. Everything was thought through, including the shape and placement of windows to create the mottled effect one would see with sunlight pouring through the branches of a thick forest. The pillars are of four different types of stone. They vary in colour and load-bearing strength, from the soft Montjuïc stone pillars along the lateral aisles through to granite, dark grey basalt and finally burgundy-tinged Iranian porphyry for the key columns at the intersection of the nave and transept. Tribunes built high above the aisles can host two choirs; the main tribune up to 1300 people and the children's tribune up to 300.

The Nativity Facade is the artistic pinnacle of the building, mostly created under Gaudí's personal supervision. You can climb high up inside some of the four towers by a combination of lifts and narrow spiral staircases – a vertiginous experience. Do not climb the stairs if you have cardiac or respiratory problems. The towers are destined to hold tubular bells capable of playing complex music at great volume. Their upper parts are decorated with mosaics spelling out 'Sanctus, Sanctus, Sanctus, Hosanna in Excelsis, Amen, Alleluia'. Asked why he lavished so much care on the tops of the spires, which no one would see from close up, Gaudí answered: 'The angels will see them'.

Three sections of the portal represent, from left to right, Hope, Charity and Faith. Among the forest of sculpture on the Charity portal you can see, low down, the manger surrounded by an ox, an ass, the shepherds and kings, and angel musicians. Some 30 different species of plant from around Catalonia are reproduced here, and the faces of the many figures are taken from plaster casts done of local people and the occasional one made from corpses in the local morgue.

Directly above the blue stained-glass window is the Archangel Gabriel's Annunciation to Mary. At the top is a green cypress tree, a refuge in a storm for the white doves of peace dotted over it. The mosaic work at the pinnacle of the towers is made from Murano glass, from Venice.

To the right of the facade is the curious Claustre del Roser, a Gothic-style mini-cloister tacked on to the outside of the church (rather than the classic square enclosure of the great Gothic church monasteries). Once inside, look back to the intricately decorated entrance. On the lower right-hand side you'll notice the sculpture of a reptilian devil handing a terrorist a bomb. Barcelona was regularly rocked by political violence and bombings were frequent in the decades prior to the civil war. The sculpture is one of several on the 'temptations of men and women'.

The southwest Passion Facade, on the theme of Christ's last days and death, was built between 1954 and 1978 based on surviving drawings by Gaudí, with four towers and a large, sculpture-bedecked portal. The sculptor, Josep Subirachs, worked on its decoration from 1986 to 2006. He did not attempt to imitate Gaudí, rather producing angular, controversial images of his own. The main series of sculptures, on three levels, are in an S-shaped sequence, starting with the Last Supper at the bottom left and ending with Christ's burial at the top right. Decorative work on the Passion Facade continues even today, as construction of the Glory Facade moves ahead.

To the right, in front of the Passion Facade, the Escoles de Gaudí is one of his simpler gems. Gaudí built this as a children's school, creating an original, undulating roof of brick that continues to charm architects to this day. Inside is a re-creation of Gaudí's modest office as it was when he died, and explanations of the geometric patterns and plans at the heart of his building techniques.

The Glory Facade is under construction and will, like the others, be crowned by four towers – the total of 12 representing the Twelve Apostles. Gaudí wanted it to be the most magnificent facade of the church. Inside will be the narthex, a kind of foyer made up of 16 'lanterns', a series of hyperboloid forms topped by cones. Further decoration will make the whole building a microcosmic symbol of the Christian church, with Christ represented by a massive 170m central tower above the transept, and the five remaining planned towers symbolising the Virgin Mary and the four evangelists.

Open the same times as the church, the Museu Gaudí, below ground level, includes interesting material on Gaudí's life and other works, as well as models and photos of La Sagrada Família. You can see a good example of his plumb-line models that showed him the stresses and strains he could get away with in construction. A side hall towards the eastern end of the museum leads to a viewing point above the simple crypt in which the genius is buried. The crypt, where Masses are now held, can also be visited from the Carrer de Mallorca side of the church.

Although essentially a building site, the completed sections and museum may be explored at leisure. Guided tours (50 minutes, €24) are offered. Alternatively, pick up an audio tour (€7), for which you need ID. Enter from Carrer de Sardenya and Carrer de la Marina. Once inside, €14 (which includes the audio tour) will get you into lifts that rise up inside the towers in the Nativity and Passion facades. These two facades, each with four sky-scraping towers, are the sides of the church. The main

Glory Facade, on which work is under way, closes off the southeast end on Carrer de Mallorca.

La Pedrera

Top choice architecture in La Sagrada Família & L'Eixample

Price - adult/concession/under 13yr/under 7yr €22/16.50/11/free

Hours - 9am-6.30pm & 7pm-9pm Mon-Sun

Contact - http://www.lapedrera.com; 902 202138

Location - Passeig de Gràcia 92, Barcelona, Spain

This undulating beast is another madcap Gaudí masterpiece, built in 1905–10 as a combined apartment and office block. Formally called Casa Milà, after the businessman who commissioned it, it is better known as La Pedrera (the Quarry) because of its uneven grey stone facade, which ripples around the corner of Carrer de Provença.

Pere Milà had married the older and far richer Roser Guardiola, the widow of Josep Guardiola, and clearly knew how to spend his new wife's money. Milà was one of the city's first car owners and Gaudí built parking space into this building, itself a first. When commissioned to design this apartment building, Gaudí wanted to top anything else done in L'Eixample.

The Fundació Caixa Catalunya has opened the top-floor apartment, attic and roof, together called the Espai Gaudí (Gaudí Space), to visitors. The roof is the most extraordinary element, with its giant chimney pots looking like multicoloured medieval knights. Short concerts are often staged up here in summer. Gaudí wanted to put a tall statue of the Virgin up here too: when the Milà family said no, fearing it might make the building a target for anarchists, Gaudí resigned from the project in disgust.

One floor below the roof, where you can appreciate Gaudí's taste for parabolic arches, is a modest museum dedicated to his work.

The next floor down is the apartment (El Pis de la Pedrera). It is fascinating to wander around this elegantly furnished home, done up in the style a well-to-do family might have enjoyed in the early 20th century. The sensuous curves and unexpected touches in everything from light fittings to bedsteads, from door handles to balconies, might seem admirable to us today, but not everyone thought so at the time. The story goes that one tenant, a certain Mrs Comes i Abril, had complained that there was no obvious place to put her piano in these wavy rooms. Gaudí's response was to suggest that she take up the flute.

For a few extra euros, a 'Premium' ticket means you don't have to queue.

Tapas 24

Top choice tapas in La Sagrada Família & L'Eixample

Price - tapas €4-9.50

Hours - 9am-midnight

Contact - http://www.carlesabellan.com; 93 488 09 77

Location - Carrer de la Diputació 269, Barcelona, Spain

Carles Abellan, master of the now-defunct Comerç 24 in La Ribera, runs this basement tapas haven known for its gourmet versions of old faves. Specials include the bikini (toasted ham and cheese sandwich – here the ham is cured and the truffle makes all the difference) and a thick black arròs negre de sípia (squid-ink black rice).

The inventive McFoie-Burger is fantastic and, for dessert, choose xocolata amb pa, sal i oli (delicious balls of chocolate in olive oil with a touch of salt and wafer). You can't book but it's worth the wait.

Museu Picasso

Top choice museum in La Ribera

Price - adult/concession/child all collections €14/7.50/free, permanent collection €11/7/free, temporary exhibitions €4.50/3/free, 6-9.30pm Thu & 1st Sun of month free

Hours - 9am-7pm Tue-Sun, to 9.30pm Thu

Contact - http://www.museupicasso.bcn.cat; 93 256 30 00

Location - Carrer de Montcada 15-23, Barcelona, Spain

The setting alone, in five contiguous medieval stone mansions, makes the Museu Picasso unique (and worth the probable queues). The pretty courtyards, galleries and staircases preserved in the first three of these buildings are as delightful as the collection inside.

While the collection concentrates on the artist's formative years – sometimes disappointing for those hoping for a feast of his better-known later works (they had better head for Paris) – there is enough material from subsequent periods to give you a thorough impression of the man's versatility and genius. Above all, you come away feeling that Picasso was the true original, always one step ahead of himself (let alone anyone else), in his search for new forms of expression.

The permanent collection is housed in Palau Aguilar, Palau del Baró de Castellet and Palau Meca, all dating to the 14th century. The 18th-century Casa Mauri, built over medieval remains (even some Roman leftovers have been identified), and the adjacent 14th-century Palau Finestres accommodate temporary exhibitions.

The collection, which includes more than 3500 artworks, is strongest on Picasso's earliest years, up until 1904, which is apt considering that the artist spent his formative creative years in Barcelona. Allegedly it was Picasso himself who proposed the museum's creation in 1960, to his friend and personal secretary Jaume Sabartés, a Barcelona native. Three years later, the 'Sabartés Collection' was opened, since a museum bearing Picasso's name would have been met with censorship – Picasso's opposition to the Franco regime was well known. The Museu Picasso we see today opened in 1983. It originally held only Sabartés' personal collection of Picasso's art and a handful of works hanging at the Barcelona Museum of Art, but the collection gradually expanded with donations from Salvador Dalí and Sebastià Junyer Vidal, among others, though the largest part of the present collection came from Picasso himself. His widow, Jacqueline Roque, also donated 41 ceramic pieces and the Woman with Bonnet painting after Picasso's death. The original collection still hangs in the Palau Aguilar.

A visit starts with sketches and oils from Picasso's earliest years in Málaga and La Coruña – around 1893–95. Some of his self-portraits and the portraits of his parents, which date from 1896, are evidence enough of his precocious talent. Retrato de la Tía Pepa (Portrait of Aunt Pepa), done in Málaga in 1896, shows the incredible maturity of his brushstrokes and his ability to portray character – at the tender age of 15! Picasso painted the enormous Ciència i caritat (Science and Charity) in the same year, showcasing his masterful academic techniques of portraiture. His ingeniousness extends to his models too, with his father standing in for the doctor, and a beggar whom he hired off the street along with her offspring, modelling the sick woman and the child. This painting caused the young artist to be noticed in the higher echelons of Spain's art world, when Ciència i caritat was awarded an Honorary Mention at the General Fine Arts Exhibition in Madrid in 1897.

In rooms 5–7 hang paintings from his first Paris sojourn, while room 8 is dedicated to the first significant new stage in his development, the Blue Period. Woman with Bonnet is an important work from this period, depicting a captive from the Saint-Lazare women's prison and venereal disease hospital that Picasso visited when in Paris – this also sets up the theme of Picasso's fascination with those inhabiting the down-and-out layers of society.

His nocturnal blue-tinted views of Terrats de Barcelona (Roofs of Barcelona) and El foll (The Madman) are cold and cheerless, yet somehow alive. Terrats de Barcelona was painted during his second stint at the 17 Carrer de la Riera Sant Joan studio in 1903 – he painted the city rooftops frequently, from different perspectives in this period. El foll shows the artist's interest in the people on the margins of society, and Picasso made many drawings of beggars, the blind and the impoverished elderly throughout 1903 and 1904.

A few cubist paintings pop up in rooms 10 and 11; check the Glass and Tobacco Packet still-life painting, a beautiful and simple work. Picasso started to experiment with still life in 1924 – something he'd done before but had not taken to as seriously as he would from here on.

From 1954 to 1962 Picasso was obsessed with the idea of researching and 'rediscovering' the greats, in particular Velázquez. In 1957 he made a series of renditions of the Velázquez' masterpiece, Las meninas, now displayed in rooms 12–14. It is as though Picasso has looked at the original Velázquez painting through a prism reflecting all the styles he had worked through until then, creating his own masterpiece in the process. This is a wonderful opportunity to see Las meninas in its entirety in this beautiful space.

The last rooms contain his dove paintings, engravings and some 40 ceramic pieces completed throughout the latter years of his unceasingly creative life. You'll see plates and bowls decorated with simple, single-line drawings of fish, owls and other animal shapes, typical for Picasso's daubing on clay.

Poble Espanyol

Cultural centre in Montjuïc, Poble Sec & Sant Antoni

Price - adult/child €14/7

Hours - 9am-8pm Mon, to midnight Tue-Thu & Sun, to 3am Fri, to 4am Sat

Contact - http://www.poble-espanyol.com

Location - Avinguda de Francesc Ferrer i Guàrdia 13, Barcelona, Spain

Welcome to Spain! All of it! This 'Spanish Village' is both a cheesy souvenir hunters' haunt and an intriguing scrapbook of Spanish architecture built for the Spanish crafts section of the 1929 World Exhibition. You can meander from Andalucía to the Balearic Islands in the space of a couple of hours, visiting surprisingly good copies of Spain's characteristic buildings.

You enter from beneath a towered medieval gate from Ávila. Inside, to the right, is an information office with free maps. Straight ahead from the gate is the Plaza Mayor (Town Sq), surrounded with mainly Castilian and Aragonese buildings. It is sometimes the scene of summer concerts. Elsewhere you'll find an Andalucian barrio (district), a Basque street, Galician and Catalan quarters, and even a Dominican monastery (at the eastern end). The buildings house dozens of restaurants, cafes, bars, craft shops and workshops (for glass artists and other artisans), and some souvenir stores.

Spare some time for the Fundació Fran Daurel, an eclectic collection of 300 works of art, including sculptures, prints, ceramics and tapestries by modern artists ranging from Picasso and Miró to more contemporary figures, such as Miquel Barceló. The foundation also has a sculpture garden, boasting 27 pieces, nearby within the grounds of Poble Espanyol (look for the Montblanc gate). Frequent temporary exhibitions broaden the offerings further.

At night the restaurants, bars and especially the discos become a lively corner of Barcelona's nightlife.

Children's groups can participate in the Joc del Sarró. Accompanied by adults, the kids go around the poble seeking the answers to various mysteries outlined in a kit distributed to each group. Languages catered for include English.

Bar Calders

Bar in Montjuïc, Poble Sec & Sant Antoni

Hours - 5pm-2am Mon-Fri, 11am-2.30am Sat, 11am-midnight Sun

Contact - 93 329 93 49

Location - Carrer del Parlament 25, Barcelona, Spain

It bills itself as a wine bar, but actually the wine selection at Bar Calders is its weak point. As an all-day cafe and tapas bar, however, it's unbeatable, with a few tables outside on a tiny pedestrian lane, and has become the favoured meeting point for the neighbourhood's boho element.

Camp Nou

Football in Camp Nou, Pedralbes & La Zona Alta

Contact - http://www.fcbarcelona.com; 902 189900

Location - Carrer d'Arístides Maillol, Barcelona, Spain

Among Barcelona's most-visited sites is the massive stadium of Camp Nou (which means New Field in Catalan), home to the legendary Futbol Club Barcelona. Attending a game amid the roar of the crowds is an unforgettable experience. Football fans who aren't able to see a game can get a taste of all the excitement at the Camp Nou Experience, which includes a visit to interactive galleries and a tour of the stadium. The season runs from September to May.

Tickets to FC Barcelona matches are available at Camp Nou, online (through FC Barcelona's official website) and through various city locations. Tourist offices sell them – the branch at Plaça de Catalunya is a centrally located option – as do FC Botiga stores. Tickets can cost anything from €39 to upwards of €250, depending on the seat and match. On match day the ticket windows (at gates 9 and 15) open from 9.15am until kick off. Tickets are not usually available for matches with Real Madrid.

You will almost definitely find scalpers lurking near the ticket windows. They are often club members and can sometimes get you in at a significant reduction. Don't pay until you are safely seated.

Park Güell

Top choice park in Gràcia & Park Güell

Price - adult/child €8/6

Hours - 8am-9.30pm May-Aug, to 8pm Sep-Apr

Contact - http://www.parkguell.cat; 93 409 18 31

Location - Carrer d'Olot 7, Barcelona, Spain

North of Gràcia and about 4km from Plaça de Catalunya, Park Güell is where Gaudí turned his hand to landscape gardening. It's a strange, enchanting place where his passion for natural forms really took flight – to the point where the artificial almost seems more natural than the natural.

Park Güell originated in 1900, when Count Eusebi Güell bought a tree-covered hillside (then outside Barcelona) and hired Gaudí to create a miniature city of houses for the wealthy in landscaped grounds. The project was a commercial flop and was abandoned in 1914 – but not before Gaudí had created 3km of roads and walks, steps, a plaza and two gatehouses in his inimitable manner. In 1922 the city bought the estate for use as a public park.

Just inside the main entrance on Carrer d'Olot, immediately recognisable by the two Hansel-and-Gretel gatehouses, is the park's Centre d'Interpretaciò, in the Pavelló de Consergeria, which is a typically curvaceous former porter's home that hosts a display on Gaudí's building methods and the history of the park. There are nice views from the top floor.

The steps up from the entrance, guarded by a mosaic dragon/lizard (a copy of which you can buy in many downtown souvenir shops), lead to the Sala Hipóstila (aka the Doric Temple). This is a forest of 88 stone columns, some of which lean like mighty trees bent by the weight of time, originally intended as a market. To the left curves a gallery whose twisted stonework columns and roof give the effect of a cloister beneath tree roots – a motif repeated in several places in the park. On top of the Sala Hipóstila is a broad open space whose centrepiece is the Banc de Trencadís, a tiled bench curving sinuously around its perimeter and designed by one of Gaudí's closest colleagues, architect Josep Maria Jujol (1879–1949). With Gaudí, however, there is always more than meets the eye. This giant platform was designed as a kind of catchment area for rainwater washing down the hillside. The water is filtered through a layer of stone and sand, and it drains down through the columns to an underground cistern.

The spired house over to the right is the Casa-Museu Gaudí, where Gaudí lived for most of his last 20 years (1906–26). It contains furniture by him (including items that were once at home in La Pedrera, Casa Batlló and Casa Calvet) and other memorabilia. The house was built in 1904 by Francesc Berenguer i Mestres as a prototype for the 60 or so houses that were originally planned here.

Much of the park is still wooded, but it's laced with pathways. The best views are from the cross-topped Turó del Calvari in the southwest corner.

The walk from metro stop Lesseps is signposted. From the Vallcarca stop, it is marginally shorter and the uphill trek eased by escalators. Bus 24 drops you at an entrance near the top of the park.

The park is extremely popular (it gets an estimated four million visitors a year, about 86% of them tourists). Access is limited to a certain number of people every half-hour, and it's wise to book ahead online (you'll also save a bit on the admission fee).

Casa Batlló

Top choice architecture in La Sagrada Família & L'Eixample

Price - adult/concession/under 7yr €23.50/20.50/free

Hours - 9am-9pm, last admission 8pm

Contact - http://www.casabatllo.es; 93 216 03 06

Location - Passeig de Gràcia 43, Barcelona, Spain

One of the strangest residential buildings in Europe, this is Gaudí at his hallucinatory best. The facade, sprinkled with bits of blue, mauve and green tiles and studded with wave-shaped window frames and balconies, rises to an uneven blue-tiled roof with a solitary tower.

It is one of the three houses on the block between Carrer del Consell de Cent and Carrer d'Aragó that gave it the playful name Manzana de la

Discordia, meaning 'Apple (Block) of Discord'. The others are Puig i Cadafalch's Casa Amatller and Domènech i Montaner's Casa Lleó Morera. They were all renovated between 1898 and 1906 and show how eclectic a 'style' Modernisme was.

Locals know Casa Batlló variously as the casa dels ossos (house of bones) or casa del drac (house of the dragon). It's easy enough to see why. The balconies look like the bony jaws of some strange beast and the roof represents Sant Jordi (St George) and the dragon. Even the roof was built to look like the shape of an animal's back, with shiny scales – the 'spine' changes colour as you walk around. If you stare long enough at the building, it seems almost to be a living being. Before going inside, take a look at the pavement. Each paving piece carries stylised images of an octopus and a starfish, designs that Gaudí originally cooked up for Casa Batlló.

When Gaudí was commissioned to refashion this building, he went to town inside and out. The internal light wells shimmer with tiles of deep sea blue. Gaudí eschewed the straight line, and so the staircase wafts you up to the 1st (main) floor, where the salon looks on to Passeig de Gràcia. Everything swirls: the ceiling is twisted into a vortex around its sunlike lamp; the doors, window and skylights are dreamy waves of wood and coloured glass. The same themes continue in the other rooms and covered terrace. The attic is characterised by Gaudí trademark hyperboloid arches. Twisting, tiled chimney pots add a surreal touch to the roof.

La Catedral

Top choice cathedral in La Rambla & Barri Gòtic

Price - free, 'donation entrance' €7, choir €3, roof €3

Hours - 8am-12.45pm & 5.15-7.30pm Mon-Fri, 8am-8pm Sat & Sun, entry by donation 1-5.30pm Mon,1-5pm Sat, 2-5pm Sun

Contact - http://www.catedralbcn.org; 93 342 82 62

Location - Plaça de la Seu, Barcelona, Spain

Barcelona's central place of worship presents a magnificent image. The richly decorated main facade, laced with gargoyles and the stone intricacies you would expect of northern European Gothic, sets it quite apart from other churches in Barcelona. The facade was actually added in 1870, although the rest of the building was built between 1298 and 1460. The other facades are sparse in decoration, and the octagonal, flat-roofed towers are a clear reminder that, even here, Catalan Gothic architectural principles prevailed.

The interior is a broad, soaring space divided into a central nave and two aisles by lines of elegant, slim pillars. The cathedral was one of the few churches in Barcelona spared by the anarchists in the civil war, so its ornamentation, never overly lavish, is intact. The faithful frequently notice the absence of holy water in the church's fonts. This is not because of a scarcity of holy water, but a preventive measure taken in the face of fear over the 2009–10 swine flu (H1N1) epidemic.

In the first chapel on the right from the northwest entrance, the main crucifixion figure above the altar is Sant Crist de Lepant. It is said Don Juan's flagship bore it into battle at Lepanto and that the figure acquired its odd stance by dodging an incoming cannonball. Further along this same wall, past the southwest transept, are the wooden coffins of Count Ramon Berenguer I and his wife Almodis, founders of the 11th-century Romanesque predecessor to the present cathedral. Left from the main entrance is the baptismal font where, according to one story, six North American Indians brought to Europe by Columbus after his first voyage of accidental discovery were bathed in holy water.

In the middle of the central nave is the late-14th-century, exquisitely sculpted timber coro (choir stalls). The coats of arms on the stalls belong to members of the Barcelona chapter of the Order of the Golden Fleece. Emperor Carlos V presided over the order's meeting here in 1519. Take the time to look at the workmanship up close – the Virgin Mary and Child depicted on the pulpit are especially fine.

A broad staircase before the main altar leads you down to the crypt, which contains the tomb of Santa Eulàlia, one of Barcelona's two patron saints and more affectionately known as Laia. The reliefs on the alabaster sarcophagus, executed by Pisan artisans, recount some of her tortures and, along the top strip, the removal of her body to its present resting place.

For a bird's-eye view (mind the poop) of medieval Barcelona, visit the cathedral's roof and tower by taking the lift (€3) from the Capella de les Animes del Purgatori near the northeast transept.

From the southwest transept, exit by the partly Romanesque door (one of the few remnants of the present church's predecessor) to the leafy claustre (cloister), with its fountains and flock of 13 geese. The geese supposedly represent the age of Santa Eulàlia at the time of her martyrdom and have, generation after generation, been squawking here since medieval days. One of the cloister chapels commemorates 930 priests, monks and nuns martyred during the civil war.

Along the northern flank of the cloister you can enter the Sala Capitular (Chapter House). Although it's bathed in rich red carpet and graced with fine timber seating, the few artworks gathered here are of minor interest. Among them figures a pietà by Bartolomeo Bermejo. A couple of doors down in the northwest corner of the cloister is the Capella de Santa Llúcia, one of the few reminders of Romanesque Barcelona (although the interior is largely Gothic). Walk out the door on to Carrer de Santa Llúcia and turn around to look at the exterior – you can see that, although incorporated into La Catedral, it is a separate building.

Upon exiting the Capella de Santa Llúcia, wander across the lane into the 16th-century Casa de l'Ardiaca, which houses the city's archives. You may stroll around the supremely serene courtyard, cooled by trees and a fountain; it was renovated by Lluis Domènech i Montaner in 1902, when the building was owned by the lawyers' college. Domènech i Montaner also designed the postal slot, which is adorned with swallows and a tortoise, said to represent the swiftness of truth and the plodding pace of justice. You can get a good glimpse at some stout Roman wall in here. Upstairs, you can look down into the courtyard and across to La Catedral.

You may visit La Catedral in one of two ways. In the morning or afternoon, entrance is free, although you have to pay to visit any combination of the choir stalls, chapter house and roof. To visit all three areas, enter via the so-called 'donation entrance' between 1pm and 5pm (which is less crowded).

Across Carrer del Bisbe is the 17th-century Palau Episcopal (Palau del Bisbat; Bishop's Palace). Virtually nothing remains of the original 13th-century structure. The Roman city's northwest gate was here and you can see the lower segments of the Roman towers that stood on either side of the gate at the base of the Palau Episcopal and Casa de l'Ardiaca. In fact, the lower part of the entire northwest wall of the Casa de l'Ardiaca is of Roman origin – you can also make out part of the first arch of a Roman aqueduct.

Across Plaça Nova from La Catedral your eye may be caught by childlike scribblings on the facade of the Col·legi de Arquitectes (Architectural College). It is, in fact, a giant contribution by Picasso from 1962. Representing Mediterranean festivals, it was much ridiculed by the local press when it was unveiled.

Museu Nacional d'Art de Catalunya

Top choice museum in Montjuïc, Poble Sec & Sant Antoni

Price - adult/student/child €12/8.40/free, after 3pm Sat & 1st Sun of month free

Hours - 10am-8pm Tue-Sat, to 3pm Sun May-Sep, to 6pm Tue-Sat Oct-Apr

Contact - http://www.museunacional.cat; 93 622 03 76

Location - Mirador del Palau Nacional, Barcelona, Spain

From across the city, the bombastic neobaroque silhouette of the Palau Nacional can be seen on the slopes of Montjuïc. Built for the 1929 World Exhibition and restored in 2005, it houses a vast collection of mostly Catalan art spanning the early Middle Ages to the early 20th century. The high point is the collection of extraordinary Romanesque frescoes.

This building has come to be one of the city's prime symbols of the region's separate, Catalan identity, but the fact that it was constructed under the centralist dictatorship of Miguel Primo de Rivera, lends a whiff of irony.

The real highlight here is the Romanesque art section, considered the most important concentration of early medieval art in the world. Rescued from neglected country churches across northern Catalonia in the early 20th century, the collection consists of 21 frescoes, woodcarvings and painted altar frontals (low-relief wooden panels that were the forerunners of the elaborate altarpieces that adorned later churches). The insides of several churches have been recreated and the frescoes – in some cases fragmentary, in others extraordinarily complete and alive with colour – have been placed as they were when in situ.

The two most striking fresco sets follow one after the other. The first, in Sala 5, is a magnificent image of Christ in Majesty done around 1123. Based on the text of the Apocalypse, we see Christ enthroned on a rainbow with the world at his feet. He holds a book open with the words Ego Sum Lux Mundi (I am the Light of the World) and is surrounded by the four Evangelists. The images were taken from the apse of the Església de Sant Climent de Taüll in northwest Catalonia. Nearby in Sala 9 are frescoes done around the same time in the nearby Església de Santa Maria de Taüll. This time the central image taken from the apse is of the Virgin Mary and Christ Child. These images were not mere decoration but tools of instruction in the basics of Christian faith for the local population – try to set yourself in the mind of the average medieval citizen: illiterate, ignorant, fearful and in most cases eking out a subsistence living. These images transmitted the basic personalities and tenets of the faith and were accepted at face value by most.

Even the rudimentary 'scratchings', done most probably by the priests, of animals, crosses and other symbols, have been rescued and preserved here.

Opposite the Romanesque collection on the ground floor is the museum's Gothic art section. In these halls you can see Catalan Gothic painting and works from other Spanish and Mediterranean regions. Look out especially for the work of Bernat Martorell in Sala 32 and Jaume Huguet in Sala 34. Among Martorell's works figure images of the martyrdom of St Vincent and St Llúcia. Huguet's Consagració de Sant Agustí, in which St Augustine is depicted as a bishop, is dazzling in its detail.

As the Gothic collection draws to a close, you pass through two separate and equally eclectic private collections. The Cambò Bequest, by Francesc Cambó (1876–1947) spans the history of European painting between the 14th century and the beginning of the 19th century, and the Thyssen-Bornemisza collection presents a selection of painting and sculpture of European art produced between the 13th and the 18th centuries on loan to the MNAC by the Museo Thyssen-Bornemisza in Madrid. The MNAC added an extra floor to absorb these two collections. Much of the work from the Cambò Bequest was kept in a Pedralbes convent before being transferred here, along with the mainly

Modernista holdings from the former Museum of Modern Art. The Thyssen-Bornemisza collection's highlight is Fra Angelico's (1395–1455) Madonna of Humility, whereas the Cambò Bequest holds wonderful works by the Venetian Renaissance masters Veronese (1528–88), Titian (1490–1557) and Canaletto (1697–1768), along with those of Rubens (1577–1640) and even England's Gainsborough (1727–88), its grand finale being examples of work by Francisco de Goya (1746–28).

From here you pass into the great domed central hall. This area is sometimes used for concerts. Up on the next floor, the collection turns to modern art, mainly but not exclusively Catalan. This collection is arranged thematically: Modernisme, Noucentisme, Art and the Civil War and so on. Among the many highlights: an early Salvador Dalí painting (Portrait of My Father), Juan Gris' collage-like paintings, the brilliant portraits of Marià Fortuny, and 1930s call-to-arms posters against the Francoist onslaught (nearby you'll find photos of soldiers and bombed-out city centres). There are also many works by Modernista painters Ramon Casas and Santiago Rusiñol, as well as Catalan luminary Antoni Tàpies.

Also on show are items of Modernista furniture and decoration, which include a mural by Ramon Casas (the artist and Pere Romeu on a tandem bicycle) that once adorned the legendary bar and restaurant Els Quatre Gats.

After all this, you can relax in the museum restaurant, which offers great views north towards Plaça d'Espanya. Finally, students can use the Biblioteca del MNAC, the city's main art reference library.

Museu d'Història de Barcelona

Top choice museum in La Rambla & Barri Gòtic

Price - adult/concession/child €7/5/free, 3-8pm Sun & 1st Sun of month free

Hours - 10am-7pm Tue-Sat, to 2pm Mon, to 8pm Sun

Contact - http://www.museuhistoria.bcn.cat; 93 256 21 00

Location - Plaça del Rei, Barcelona, Spain

One of Barcelona's most fascinating museums takes you back through the centuries to the very foundations of Roman Barcino. You'll stroll over ruins of the old streets, sewers, laundries and wine- and fish-making factories that flourished here following the town's founding by Emperor Augustus around 10 BC. Equally impressive is the building itself, which was once part of the Palau Reial Major (Grand Royal Palace) on Plaça del Rei, among the key locations of medieval princely power in Barcelona.

The square is frequently the scene of organised or impromptu concerts and is one of the most atmospheric corners of the medieval city.

Enter through Casa Padellàs, just south of Plaça del Rei. Casa Padellàs was built for a 16th-century noble family in Carrer dels Mercaders and moved here, stone by stone, in the 1930s. It has a courtyard typical of Barcelona's late-Gothic and baroque mansions, with a graceful external staircase up to the 1st floor. Today it leads to a restored Roman tower and a section of Roman wall (whose exterior faces Plaça Ramon de Berenguer el Gran), as well as a section of the house set aside for temporary exhibitions.

Below ground is a remarkable walk through about 4 sq km of excavated Roman and Visigothic Barcelona. After the display on the typical Roman domus (villa), you reach a public laundry (outside in the street were containers for people to urinate into, as the urine was used as disinfectant). You pass more laundries and dyeing shops, a 6th-century public cold-water bath and more dye shops. As you hit the Cardo Minor (a main street), you turn right then left and reach various shops dedicated to the making of garum. This paste, a fave food across the Roman Empire, was made of mashed-up fish intestines, eggs and blood. Occasionally prawns, cockles and herbs were added to create other flavours. Further on are fish-preserve stores. Fish were sliced up (and all innards removed for making garum), laid in alternate layers using salt for preservation, and sat in troughs for about three weeks before being ready for sale and export.

Next come remnants of a 6th- to 7th-century church and episcopal buildings, followed by winemaking stores, with ducts for allowing the must to flow off, and ceramic, round-bottomed dolia for storing and ageing wine. Ramparts then wind around and upward, past remains of the gated patio of a Roman house, the medieval Palau Episcopal (Bishops' Palace) and into two broad vaulted halls with displays on medieval Barcelona.

You eventually emerge at a hall and ticket office set up on the north side of Plaça del Rei. To your right is the Saló del Tinell, the banqueting hall of the royal palace and a fine example of Catalan Gothic (built 1359–70). Its broad arches and bare walls give a sense of solemnity that would have made an appropriate setting for Fernando and Isabel to hear Columbus' first reports of the New World. The hall is sometimes used for temporary exhibitions, which may cost extra and mean that your peaceful contemplation of its architectural majesty is somewhat obstructed.

As you leave the saló you come to the 14th-century Capella Reial de Santa Àgata, the palace chapel. Outside, a spindly bell tower rises from the northeast side of Plaça del Rei. Inside, all is bare except for the 15th-century altarpiece and the magnificent techumbre (decorated timber ceiling). The altarpiece is considered to be one of Jaume Huguet's finest surviving works.

Head down the fan-shaped stairs into Plaça del Rei and look up to observe the Mirador del Rei Martí (lookout tower of King Martin), built in 1555, long after the king's death. It is part of the Arxiu de la Corona d'Aragón; the magnificent views over the old city are now enjoyed only by a privileged few.

Entry here includes admission to other MUHBA-run sites, such as the Domus de Sant Honorat and the MUHBA Refugi 307.

Madrid

No city on earth is more alive than Madrid, a beguiling place whose sheer energy carries a simple message: this city really knows how to live.

An Artistic City

Few cities boast an artistic pedigree quite as pure as Madrid's: many art lovers return here again and again. For centuries, Spanish royals showered praise and riches upon the finest artists of the day, from home-grown talents such as Goya and Velázquez to Flemish and Italian greats. Masterpieces by these and other Spanish painters such as Picasso, Dalí and Miró now adorn the walls of the city's world-class galleries. Three in particular are giants – the Museo del Prado, Centro de Arte Reina Sofía and Museo Thyssen-Bornemisza – but in Madrid these are merely good places to start.

A Culinary Capital

Rising above the humble claims of its local cuisine, Madrid has evolved into one of the richest culinary capitals of Europe. The city has wholeheartedly embraced all the creativity and innovation of Spain's gastronomic revolution. But this acceptance of the new is wedded to a passion for the enduring traditions of Spanish cooking, for the conviviality of the eating experience and for showcasing the infinite variety of food from every Spanish region. From tapas in sleek temples to all that's new to sit-down meals beneath centuries-old vaulted ceilings, eating in Madrid is a genuine pleasure.

Killing the Night

Madrid nights are the stuff of legend, and the perfect complement to the more sedate charms of fine arts and fine dining. The city may have more bars than any other city on earth – a collection of storied cocktail bars and nightclubs that combine a hint of glamour with non-stop marcha (action). But that only goes some way to explaining the appeal of after-dark Madrid. Step out into the night-time streets of many Madrid neighbourhoods and you'll find yourself swept along on a tide of people, accompanied by a happy crowd intent on dancing until dawn.

Beautiful Architecture

Madrid may lack the cachet of Paris, the monumental history of Rome, or Barcelona's reputation for Modernista masterpieces. And no, there is no equivalent of the Eiffel Tower, Colosseum or La Sagrada Família that you can point to and say 'this is Madrid'. But Madrid has nothing to be envious of. Spain's broad sweep of architectural history provides a glorious backdrop to city life, from medieval mansions and royal palaces to the unimagined angles of Spanish contemporary architecture, from the sober brickwork and slate spires of Madrid baroque to the extravagant confections of the belle époque. Put simply, this is one beautiful city.

Experiences in Madrid

Museo del Prado

Top choice museum in El Retiro & the Art Museums

Price - adult/child €15/free, 6-8pm Mon-Sat & 5-7pm Sun free, audio guides €3.50, admission plus official guidebook €24

Hours - 10am-8pm Mon-Sat, 10am-7pm Sun

Contact - http://www.museodelprado.es

Location - Paseo del Prado, Madrid, Spain

Welcome to one of the world's premier art galleries. The more than 7000 paintings held in the Museo del Prado's collection (although only around 1500 are currently on display) are like a window onto the historical vagaries of the Spanish soul, at once grand and imperious in the royal paintings of Velázquez, darkly tumultuous in Las pinturas negras (The Black Paintings) of Goya, and outward looking with sophisticated works of art from all across Europe.

Spend as long as you can at the Prado or, better still, plan to make a couple of visits because it can be a little overwhelming if you try to absorb it all at once.

Entrance to the Prado is via the eastern Puerta de los Jerónimos, with tickets on sale beneath the northern Puerta de Goya. Once inside, pick up the free plan from the ticket office or information desk just inside the entrance – it lists the locations of 50 of the Prado's most famous works and gives room numbers for all major artists.

History

The western wing of the Prado (Edificio Villanueva) was completed in 1785, as the neoclassical Palacio de Villanueva. Originally conceived as a house of science, it later served, somewhat ignominiously, as a cavalry barracks for Napoleon's troops during their occupation of Madrid between 1808 and 1813. In 1814 King Fernando VII decided to use the palace as a museum, although his purpose was more about finding a way of storing the hundreds of royal paintings gathering dust than any high-minded civic ideals – this was an era where art was a royal preserve. Five years later the Museo del Prado opened with 311 Spanish paintings on display.

Goya

Francisco José de Goya y Lucientes (Goya) is found on all three floors of the Prado, but we recommend starting at the southern end of the ground or lower level. In Room 65, Goya's El dos de mayo and El tres de mayo rank among Madrid's most emblematic paintings; they bring to life the 1808 anti-French revolt and subsequent execution of insurgents in Madrid. Alongside, in Rooms 67 and 68, are some of his darkest and most disturbing works, Las pinturas negras; they are so called in part because of the dark browns and black that dominate, but more for the distorted animalesque appearance of their characters.

There are more Goyas on the 1st floor in Rooms 34 to 37. Among them are two more of Goya's best-known and most intriguing oils: La maja vestida and La maja desnuda. These portraits, in Room 37, of an unknown woman, commonly believed to be the Duquesa de Alba (who may have been Goya's lover), are identical save for the lack of clothing in the latter. There are further Goyas on the top floor.

Velázquez

Diego Rodriguez de Silva y Velázquez (Velázquez) is another of the grand masters of Spanish art who brings so much distinction to the Prado. Of all his works, Las meninas (Room 12) is what most people come to see. Completed in 1656, it is more properly known as La família de Felipe IV (The Family of Felipe IV). The rooms surrounding Las meninas contain more fine works by Velázquez: watch in particular for his paintings of various members of royalty who seem to spring off the canvas – Felipe II, Felipe IV, Margarita de Austria (a younger version of whom features in Las meninas), El Príncipe Baltasar Carlos and Isabel de Francia – on horseback.

Spanish & Other European Masters

Having experienced the essence of the Prado, you're now free to select from the astonishingly diverse works that remain. If Spanish painters have piqued your curiosity, Bartolomé Esteban Murillo, José de Ribera and the stark figures of Francisco de Zurbarán should be on your itinerary. The vivid, almost-surreal works by the 16th-century master and adopted Spaniard El Greco, whose figures are characteristically slender and tortured, are also perfectly executed.

Another alternative is the Prado's outstanding collection of Flemish art. The fulsome figures and bulbous cherubs of Peter Paul Rubens (1577–1640) provide a playful antidote to the darkness of many of the other Flemish artists. His signature works are Las tres gracias (The Three Graces) and Adoración de los reyes magos. Other fine works in the vicinity include The Triumph of Death by Pieter Bruegel, Rembrandt's Artemisa,and those by Anton Van Dyck. And on no account miss the weird and wonderful The Garden of Earthly Delights (Room 56A) by Hieronymus Bosch (c 1450–1516). No one has yet been able to provide a definitive explanation for this hallucinatory work, although many have tried.

And then there are the paintings by Dürer, Rafael, Tiziano (Titian), Tintoretto, Sorolla, Gainsborough, Fra Angelico, Tiepolo…

Edificio Jerónimos

In contrast to the original Edificio Villanueva, the eastern wing (Edificio Jerónimos) is part of the Prado's stunning modern extension, which opened in 2007. Dedicated to temporary exhibitions (usually to display Prado masterpieces held in storage for decades for lack of wall space), and home to the excellent bookshop and cafe, its main attraction is the 2nd-floor cloisters. Built in 1672 with local granite, the cloisters were until recently attached to the adjacent Iglesia de San Jerónimo El Real, but were in a parlous state. As part of their controversial incorporation into the Prado, they were painstakingly dismantled, restored and reassembled.

Plaza Mayor

Top choice square in Plaza Mayor & Royal Madrid

Madrid's grand central square, a rare but expansive opening in the tightly packed streets of central Madrid, is one of the prettiest open spaces in Spain, a winning combination of imposing architecture, picaresque historical tales and vibrant street life coursing across its cobblestones. At once beautiful in its own right and a reference point for so many Madrid days, it also hosts the city's main tourist office, a Christmas market in December and arches leading to laneways leading out into the labyrinth.

Ah, the history the plaza has seen! Designed in 1619 by Juan Gómez de Mora and built in typical Herrerian style, of which the slate spires are the most obvious expression, its first public ceremony was suitably auspicious – the beatification of San Isidro Labrador (St Isidro the Farm Labourer), Madrid's patron saint. Thereafter it was as if all that was controversial about Spain took place in this square. Bullfights, often in celebration of royal weddings or births, with royalty watching on from the balconies and up to 50,000 people crammed into the plaza, were a recurring theme until 1878. Far more notorious were the autos-da-fé (the ritual condemnations of heretics during the Spanish Inquisition), followed by executions – burnings at the stake and deaths by garrotte on the north side of the square, hangings to the south. These continued until 1790 when a fire largely destroyed the square, which was subsequently reproduced under the supervision of Juan de Villanueva, who lent his name to the building that now houses the Museo del Prado. These days, the plaza is an epicentre of Madrid life.

The grandeur of the plaza is due in large part to the warm colours of the uniformly ochre apartments, with 237 wrought-iron balconies offset by the exquisite frescoes of the 17th-century Real Casa de la Panadería (Royal Bakery). The present frescoes date to just 1992 and are the work of artist Carlos Franco, who chose images from the signs of the zodiac and gods (eg Cybele) to provide a stunning backdrop for the plaza. The frescoes were inaugurated to coincide with Madrid's 1992 spell as European Capital of Culture.

Centro de Arte Reina Sofía

Top choice museum in El Retiro & the Art Museums

Price - adult/concession €10/free, 1.30-7pm Sun, 7-9pm Mon & Wed-Sat free

Hours - 10am-9pm Mon & Wed-Sat, 10am-7pm Sun

Contact - http://www.museoreinasofia.es; 91 774 10 00

Location - Calle de Santa Isabel 52, Madrid, Spain

Home to Picasso's Guernica, arguably Spain's most famous artwork, the Centro de Arte Reina Sofía is Madrid's premier collection of contemporary art. In addition to plenty of paintings by Picasso, other major drawcards are works by Salvador Dalí (1904–89) and Joan Miró (1893–1983). The collection principally spans the 20th century up to the

1980s. The occasional non-Spaniard artist makes an appearance (including Francis Bacon's Lying Figure; 1966), but most of the collection is strictly peninsular.

The permanent collection is displayed on the 2nd and 4th floors of the main wing of the museum, the Edificio Sabatini. Guernica's location never changes – you'll find it in Room 206 on the 2nd floor. Beyond that, the location of specific paintings can be a little confusing. The museum follows a theme-based approach, which ensures that you'll find works by Picasso or Miró, for example, spread across the two floors. The only solution if you're looking for something specific is to pick up the latest copy of the Planos de Museo (Museum Floorplans) from the information desk just outside the main entrance; it lists the rooms in which each artist appears (although not individual paintings).

In addition to Picasso's Guernica, which is worth the admission fee on its own, don't neglect the artist's preparatory sketches in the rooms surrounding Room 206; they offer an intriguing insight into the development of this seminal work. If Picasso's cubist style has captured your imagination, the work of the Madrid-born Juan Gris (1887–1927) or Georges Braque (1882–1963) may appeal.

The work of Joan Miró is defined by often delightfully bright primary colours, but watch out also for a handful of his equally odd sculptures. Since his paintings became a symbol of the Barcelona Olympics in 1992, his work has begun to receive the international acclaim it so richly deserves – the museum is a fine place to get a representative sample of his innovative work.

The Reina Sofía is also home to 20 or so canvases by Salvador Dalí, of which the most famous is perhaps the surrealist extravaganza that is El gran masturbador (1929). Among his other works is a strange bust of a certain Joelle, which Dalí created with his friend Man Ray (1890–1976). Another well-known surrealist painter, Max Ernst (1891–1976), is also worth tracking down.

If you can tear yourself away from the big names, the Reina Sofía offers a terrific opportunity to learn more about sometimes lesser-known 20th-century Spanish artists. Among these are Miquel Barceló (b 1957); madrileño artist José Gutiérrez Solana (1886–1945); the renowned Basque painter Ignazio Zuloaga (1870–1945); Benjamín Palencia (1894–1980), whose paintings capture the turbulence of Spain in the 1930s; Barcelona painter Antoni Tàpies (1923–2012); pop artist Eduardo Arroyo (b 1937); and abstract painters such as Eusebio Sempere (1923–85) and members of the Equipo 57 group (founded in 1957 by a group of Spanish artists in exile in Paris), such as Pablo Palazuelo (1916–2007). Better known as a poet and playwright, Federico García Lorca (1898–1936) is represented by a number of his sketches.

Of the sculptors, watch in particular for Pablo Gargallo (1881–1934), whose work in bronze includes a bust of Picasso, and the renowned Basque sculptors Jorge Oteiza (1908–2003) and Eduardo Chillida (1924–2002).

Basílica de San Francisco El Grande

Top choice church in La Latina & Lavapiés

Price - adult/concession €5/3

Hours - mass 8-10.30am Mon-Sat, museum 10.30am-12.30pm & 4-6pm Tue-Sun Sep-Jun, 10.30am-12.30pm & 5-7pm Tue-Sun Jul & Aug

Location - Plaza de San Francisco 1, Madrid, Spain

Lording it over the southwestern corner of La Latina, this imposing baroque basilica is one of Madrid's grandest old churches. Its extravagantly frescoed dome is, by some estimates, the largest in Spain and the fourth largest in the world, with a height of 56m and diameter of 33m.

Legend has it that St Francis of Assisi built a chapel on this site in 1217. The current version was designed by Francesco Sabatini, who also designed the Puerta de Alcalá and finished off the Palacio Real. He designed the church with an unusual floor plan: the nave is circular and surrounded by chapels guarded by imposing marble statues of the 12 apostles; 12 prophets, rendered in wood, sit above them at the base of the dome. Each of the chapels is adorned with frescoes and decorated according to a different historical style, but most people rush to the neo-plateresque Capilla de San Bernardino, where the central fresco was painted by Goya in the early stages of his career. Unusually, Goya has painted himself into the scene (he's the one in the yellow shirt on the right).

A series of corridors behind the high altar (accessible only as part of the guided visit) is lined with works of art from the 17th to 19th centuries; highlights include a painting by Francisco Zurbarán, and another by Francisco Pacheco, the father-in-law and teacher of Velázquez. In the sacristy, watch out for the fine Renaissance sillería (the sculpted walnut seats where the church's superiors would meet).

A word about the opening hours: although entry is free during morning Mass times, there is no access to the museum and the lights in the Capilla de San Bernardino won't be on to illuminate the Goya. At all other times, visit is by Spanish-language guided tour (included in the admission Price). Just to confuse matters, you may face a similar problem if you're here on a Friday afternoon or any time Saturday if there's a wedding taking place.

Museo Thyssen-Bornemisza

Top choice museum in El Retiro & the Art Museums

Price - adult/child €12/free, Mon free

Hours - 10am-7pm Tue-Sun, noon-4pm Mon

Contact - http://www.museothyssen.org; 902 760511

Location - Paseo del Prado 8, Madrid, Spain

The Thyssen is one of the most extraordinary private collections of predominantly European art in the world. Where the Prado or Reina Sofía enable you to study the body of work of a particular artist in depth, the Thyssen is the place to immerse yourself in a breathtaking breadth of artistic styles. Most of the big names are here, sometimes with just a single painting, but the Thyssen's gift to Madrid and the art-loving public is to have them all under one roof.

Begin on the top floor and work your way down.

Second Floor

The 2nd floor, which is home to medieval art, includes some real gems hidden among the mostly 13th- and 14th-century and predominantly Italian, German and Flemish religious paintings and triptychs. Unless you've got a specialist's eye, pause in Room 5, where you'll find one work by Italy's Piero della Francesca (1410–92) and the instantly recognisable Portrait of King Henry VIII by Holbein the Younger (1497–1543), before continuing on to Room 10 for the evocative 1586 Massacre of the Innocents by Lucas Van Valckenberch. Room 11 is dedicated to El Greco (with three pieces) and his Venetian contemporaries Tintoretto and Titian, while Caravaggio and the Spaniard José de Ribera dominate Room 12. A single painting each by Murillo and Zurbarán add further Spanish flavour in the two rooms that follow, while the exceptionally rendered views of Venice by Canaletto (1697–1768) should on no account be missed.

Best of all on this floor is the extension (Rooms A to H) built to house the collection of Carmen Thyssen-Bornemisza. Room C houses paintings by Canaletto, Constable and Van Gogh, while the stunning Room H includes works by Monet, Sisley, Renoir, Pissarro and Degas.

Before heading downstairs, a detour to Rooms 19 through 21 will satisfy those devoted to 17th-century Dutch and Flemish masters, such as Anton van Dyck, Jan Brueghel the Elder, Rubens and Rembrandt (one painting).

First Floor

If all that sounds impressive, the 1st floor is where the Thyssen really shines. There's a Gainsborough in Room 28 and a Goya in Room 31 but, if you've been skimming the surface of this overwhelming collection, Room 32 is the place to linger over each and every painting. The astonishing texture of Van Gogh's Les Vessenots is a masterpiece, but the same could be said for Woman in Riding Habit by Manet, The Thaw at Véthueil by Monet, Renoir's Woman with a Parasol in a Garden and Pissarro's quintessentially Parisian Rue Saint-Honoré in the Afternoon. Room 33 is also something special, with Cézanne, Gauguin, Toulouse-Lautrec and Degas, while the big names continue in Room 34 (Picasso, Matisse and Modigliani) and 35 (Edvard Munch and Egon Schiele).

In the 1st floor's extension (Rooms I to P), the names speak for themselves. Room K has works by Monet, Pissaro, Sorolla and Sisley, while Room L is the domain of Gauguin (including his iconic Mata Mua), Degas and Toulouse-Lautrec. Rooms M (Munch), N (Kandinsky), O (Matisse and Georges Braque) and P (Picasso, Matisse, Edward Hopper and Juan Gris) round out an outrageously rich journey through the masters. On your way to the stairs there's Edward Hopper's Hotel Room.

Ground Floor

On the ground floor, the foray into the 20th century that you began in the 1st-floor extension takes over with a fine spread of paintings from cubism through to pop art.

In Room 41 you'll see a nice mix of the big three of cubism, Picasso, Georges Braque and Madrid's own Juan Gris, along with several other contemporaries. Kandinsky is the main drawcard in Room 43, while there's an early Salvador Dalí alongside Max Ernst and Paul Klee in

Room 44. Picasso appears again in Room 45, another one of the gallery's standout rooms; its treasures include works by Marc Chagall and Dalí's hallucinatory Dream Caused by the Flight of a Bee Around a Pomegranate, One Second Before Waking Up.

Room 46 is similarly rich, with Joan Miró's Catalan Peasant with a Guitar, the splattered craziness of Jackson Pollock's Brown and Silver I, and the deceptively simple but strangely pleasing Green on Maroon by Mark Rothko taking centre stage. In Rooms 47 and 48 the Thyssen builds to a stirring climax, with Francis Bacon, Roy Lichtenstein, Henry Moore and Lucian Freud, Sigmund's Berlin-born grandson, all represented.

Parque del Buen Retiro

Top choice gardens in El Retiro & the Art Museums

Hours - 6am-midnight May-Sep, to 10pm Oct-Apr

Location - Plaza de la Independencia, Madrid, Spain

The glorious gardens of El Retiro are as beautiful as any you'll find in a European city. Littered with marble monuments, landscaped lawns, the occasional elegant building (the Palacio de Cristal is especially worth seeking out) and abundant greenery, it's quiet and contemplative during the week but comes to life on weekends. Put simply, this is one of our favourite places in Madrid.

Laid out in the 17th century by Felipe IV as the preserve of kings, queens and their intimates, the park was opened to the public in 1868 and ever since, whenever the weather's fine and on weekends in particular, madrileños (people from Madrid) from all across the city gather here to stroll, read the Sunday papers in the shade, take a boat ride or nurse a cool drink at the numerous outdoor terrazas (open-air cafes).

The focal point for so much of El Retiro's life is the artificial lake (estanque), which is watched over by the massive ornamental structure of the Monument to Alfonso XII on the east side, complete with marble lions; as sunset approaches on a Sunday afternoon in summer, the crowd grows, bongos sound out across the park and people start to dance. Row boats can be rented from the lake's northern shore – an iconic Madrid experience. On the southern end of the lake, the odd structure decorated with sphinxes is the Fuente Egipcia: legend has it that an enormous fortune buried in the park by Felipe IV in the mid-18th century rests here. Hidden among the trees south of the lake is the Palacio de Cristal, a magnificent metal-and-glass structure that is arguably El Retiro's most beautiful architectural monument. It was built in 1887 as a winter garden for exotic flowers and is now used for temporary exhibitions organised by the Centro de Arte Reina Sofía. Just north of here, the 1883 Palacio de Velázquez is also used for temporary exhibitions.

At the southern end of the park, near La Rosaleda (Rose Garden) with its more than 4000 roses, is a statue of El Ángel Caído. Strangely, it sits 666m above sea level… In the same vein, the Puerta de Dante, in the extreme southeastern corner of the park, is watched over by a carved mural of Dante's Inferno. Occupying much of the southwestern corner of the park is the Jardín de los Planteles, one of the least visited sections of El Retiro, where quiet pathways lead beneath an overarching canopy of trees. West of here is the moving Bosque del Recuerdo, an understated memorial to the 191 victims of the 11 March 2004 train bombings. For each victim stands an olive or cypress tree. To the north, just inside the Puerta de Felipe IV, stands what is thought to be Madrid's oldest tree, a Mexican conifer (ahuehuete) planted in 1633.

In the northeastern corner of the park is the Ermita de San Isidro, a small country chapel noteworthy as one of the few, albeit modest, examples of Romanesque architecture in Madrid. When it was built, Madrid was a small village more than 2km away.

Museo Lázaro Galdiano

Top choice museum in Salamanca

Price - adult/concession/child €6/3/free, last hour free

Hours - 10am-4.30pm Mon & Wed-Sat, 10am-3pm Sun

Contact - http://www.flg.es; 91 561 60 84

Location - Calle de Serrano 122, Madrid, Spain

This imposing early 20th-century Italianate stone mansion, set discreetly back from the street, belonged to Don José Lázaro Galdiano (1862–1947), a successful businessman and passionate patron of the arts. His astonishing private collection, which he bequeathed to the city upon his death, includes 13,000 works of art and objets d'art, a quarter of which are on show at any time.

It can be difficult to believe the breadth of masterpieces that Señor Lázaro Galdiano gathered during his lifetime, and there's enough here to merit this museum's inclusion among Madrid's best art galleries. The highlights include works by Zurbarán, Claudio Coello, Hieronymus Bosch, Esteban Murillo, El Greco, Lucas Cranach and John Constable, and there's even a painting in Room 11 attributed to Velázquez.

As is often the case, Goya belongs in a class of his own. He dominates Room 13, while the ceiling of the adjoining Room 14 features a collage from some of Goya's more famous works. Some that are easy to recognise include La maja desnuda, La maja vestida and the frescoes of the Ermita de San Antonio de la Florida.

The ground floor is largely given over to a display setting the social context in which Galdiano lived, with hundreds of curios from all around the world on show. This remarkable collection ranges beyond paintings to sculptures, bronzes, miniature figures, jewellery, ceramics, furniture, weapons...clearly he was a man of wide interests. The lovely 1st floor is dominated by Spanish artworks arrayed around the centrepiece of the former ballroom and beneath lavishly frescoed ceilings. The 2nd floor contains numerous minor masterpieces from Italian, Flemish, English and French painters, while the top floor is jammed with all sorts of ephemera, including some exquisite textiles in Room 24.

The labelling throughout the museum is excellent, appearing in both English and Spanish, and is accompanied by photos of each room as it appeared in Galdiano's prime.

Born in Navarra in northeastern Spain, José Lázaro Galdiano moved to Madrid as a young man. He would later become a hugely significant figure in the cultural life of the city. During WWI he was an important supporter of the Museo del Prado, and later built his own private collection by buying up Spanish artworks in danger of being sold overseas and bringing home those that had already left. He lived in exile during the Civil War, but continued to collect and upon his return he set up a respected artistic foundation in his former palace that would ultimately house the museum.

Real Academia de Bellas Artes de San Fernando

Top choice museum in Sol, Santa Ana & Huertas

Price - adult/child €6/free, Wed free

Hours - 10am-3pm Tue-Sun Sep-Jul

Contact - http://www.realacademiabellasartessanfernando.com; 91 524 08 64

Location - Calle de Alcalá 13, Madrid, Spain

Madrid's 'other' art gallery, the Real Academia de Bellas Artes has for centuries played a pivotal role in the artistic life of the city. As the royal fine arts academy, it has nurtured local talent, thereby complementing the royal penchant for drawing the great international artists of the day into their realm. The pantheon of former alumni reads like a who's who of Spanish art, and the collection that now hangs on the academy's walls is a suitably rich one.

In any other city, this gallery would be a stand-out attraction, but in Madrid it often gets forgotten in the rush to the Prado, Thyssen or Reina Sofía. Nonetheless a visit here is a fascinating journey into another age of art; when we tell you that Picasso and Dalí studied at this academy (long the academic centre of learning for up-and-coming artists), but found it far too stuffy for their liking, you'll get an idea of what to expect. A centre of excellence since Fernando VI founded the academy in the 18th century, it remains a stunning repository of works by some of the best-loved old masters.

The 1st floor, mainly devoted to 16th- to 19th-century paintings, is the most noteworthy of those in the academic gallery. Among relative unknowns, you come across a hall of works by Zurbarán (especially arresting is the series of full-length portraits of white-cloaked friars) and a San Jerónimo by El Greco.

At a 'fork' in the exhibition, a sign points right to rooms 11 to 16, the main one showcasing Alonso Cano (1601–67) and José de Ribera (1591–1652). In the others a couple of minor portraits by Velázquez hang alongside the occasional Rubens, Tintoretto and Bellini, which have somehow been smuggled in. Rooms 17 to 22 offer a space full of Bravo Murillo and last, but most captivating, 13 pieces by Goya, including self-portraits, portraits of King Fernando VII and the infamous minister Manuel Godoy, along with one on bullfighting.

The 19th and 20th centuries are the themes upstairs. It's not the most extensive or engaging modern collection, but you'll find drawings by Picasso as well as works by Joaquín Sorolla, Juan Gris, Eduardo Chillida and Ignacio Zuloaga, in most cases with only one or two items each.

Valencia

Spain's third-largest city is a magnificent place, content for Madrid and Barcelona to grab the headlines while it gets on with being a wonderfully liveable city with thriving cultural, eating and nightlife scenes. Never afraid to innovate, Valencia diverted its flood-prone river to the outskirts of town and converted the former riverbed into a superb green ribbon of park winding right through the city. On it are the strikingly futuristic buildings of the Ciudad de las Artes y las Ciencias, designed by local boy Santiago Calatrava. Other brilliant contemporary buildings grace the city, which also has a fistful of fabulous Modernista architecture, great museums and a large, characterful old quarter. Valencia, surrounded by its huerta, a fertile fruit-and-veg farmland, is famous as the home of rice dishes such as paella, but its buzzy dining scene offers plenty more besides.

Experiences in Valencia

Ciudad de las Artes y las Ciencias

Notable building in L'Eixample & Southern Valencia

Contact - http://www.cac.es; 902 100031

Location - Valencia, Spain

The aesthetically stunning City of Arts & Sciences occupies a massive 350,000-sq-metre swath of the old Turia riverbed. It's mostly the work of world-famous, locally born architect Santiago Calatrava. He's a controversial figure for many Valencians, who complain about the expense, and various design flaws that have necessitated major repairs here. Nevertheless, if your taxes weren't involved, it's awe-inspiring stuff, and pleasingly family-oriented.

Navarro

Top choice valencian in South Ciutat Vella

Price - rices €11-18, set menu €22

Hours - 1.30-4pm daily, 8.30-11pm Sat

Contact - http://www.restaurantenavarro.com; 963 52 96 23

Location - Calle del Arzobispo Mayoral 5, Valencia, Spain

A byword in the city for decades for their quality rice dishes, Navarro is run by the grandkids of the original founders and it offers plenty of choice, outdoor seating and a set menu, including one of the rices as a main.

La Lonja

Top choice historic building in North Ciutat Vella

Price - adult/child €2/1, Sun free

Hours - 9.30am-7pm Mon-Sat, 9.30am-3pm Sun

Contact - http://www.valencia.es; 962 08 41 53

Location - Calle de la Lonja, Valencia, Spain

This splendid building, a Unesco World Heritage site, was originally Valencia's silk and commodity exchange, built in the late 15th century when Valencia was booming. It's one of Spain's finest examples of a civil Gothic building. Two main structures flank a citrus-studded courtyard: the magnificent Sala de Contratación, a cathedral of commerce with soaring twisted pillars, and the Consulado del Mar, where a maritime tribunal sat. The top floor boasts a stunning coffered ceiling brought here from another building.

It's worth getting the audio guide (€3) as there's almost no printed information. The exterior (covered by the audio guide) also merits examination.

Mercado Central

Top choice market in North Ciutat Vella

Hours - 7.30am-3pm Mon-Sat

Contact - http://www.mercadocentralvalencia.es; 963 82 91 00

Location - Plaza del Mercado, Valencia, Spain

Valencia's vast Modernista covered market, constructed in 1928, is a swirl of smells, movement and colour. Spectacular seafood counters display cephalopods galore and numerous fish species, while the fruit and vegetables, many produced locally in Valencia's huerta (area of market gardens), are of special quality. A tapas bar lets you sip a wine and enjoy the atmosphere.

Catedral

Top choice cathedral in North Ciutat Vella

Price - adult/child incl audio guide €7/5.50

Hours - 10am-6.30pm Mon-Sat, 2-5.30pm Sun, to 5.30pm Nov-Mar, closed Sun Nov-Feb

Contact - http://www.catedraldevalencia.es; 963 91 81 27

Location - Plaza de la Virgen, Valencia, Spain

Valencia's cathedral was built over the mosque after the 1238 reconquest. Its low, wide, brick-vaulted triple nave is mostly Gothic, with neoclassical side chapels. Highlights are rich Italianate frescoes above the altarpiece, a pair of Goyas in the Capilla de San Francisco de Borja, and…ta-dah…in the flamboyant Gothic Capilla del Santo Cáliz, what's claimed to be the Holy Grail from which Christ sipped during the Last Supper. It's a Roman-era agate cup, later modified, so at least the date is right.

Various relics and a beautiful transitional altarpiece in the Capilla de San Dionisio are other noteworthy features.

Left of the main portal is the entrance to the bell tower El Miguelete. Climb the 207 steps of its spiral staircase for terrific 360-degree city-and-skyline views.

As done for over a thousand years, the Tribunal de las Aguas (Water Court) meets every Thursday exactly at noon outside the cathedral's Puerta de los Apóstoles. Here, Europe's oldest legal institution settles local farmers' irrigation disputes in Valenciano, the regional language.

Museo de Bellas Artes

Top choice gallery in Northern & Eastern Valencia

Hours - 10am-8pm Tue-Sun

Contact - http://www.museobellasartesvalencia.gva.es; 963 87 03 00

Location - Calle de San Pío V 9, Valencia, Spain

Bright and spacious, this gallery ranks among Spain's best. Highlights include a collection of magnificent late-medieval altarpieces, and works by several Spanish masters, including some great Goya portraits, a haunting Velázquez selfie, an El Greco John the Baptist, Murillos, Riberas and works by the Ribaltas, father and son. Downstairs, an excellent series of rooms focuses on the great, versatile Valencian painter Joaquín Sorolla (1863–1923), who, at his best, seemed to capture the spirit of an age through sensitive portraiture.

Museo Nacional de Cerámica

Top choice museum in South Ciutat Vella

Price - adult/child €3/free, Sat afternoon & Sun free

Hours - 10am-2pm & 4-8pm Tue-Sat, 10am-2pm Sun

Contact - http://www.mecd.gob.es; 963 08 54 29

Location - Calle del Poeta Querol 2, Valencia, Spain

Inside a striking palace, this ceramics museum celebrates an important Valencia-region industry. Downstairs (if you can take your eyes off a decadent hand-painted 1753 carriage) you can learn about the history of ceramics from baroque to modern, with great information that's albeit sometimes a little difficult to relate to the pottery on display. Upstairs, historical ceramics are cleverly dotted with modern works, but the sumptuous, over-the-top interiors, all ornate stucco, chinoiserie, damask panels and elaborate upholstery, pull plenty of focus. It's an outrageous rococo extravaganza.

Look out for a fabulous painted ceiling from the original building. The modern top floor has details on ceramics production and a porcelain collection from the Alcora factory, which, along with Manises and Paterna, was an important local production centre. Porcelain and other ceramics are still huge in the Valencian region.

Museo del Patriarca

Top choice gallery in South Ciutat Vella

Price - €2

Hours - 11am-1.30pm daily, also often 5-7pm Mon-Fri

Location - Calle de la Nave 1, Valencia, Spain

This seminary was founded in the late 16th-century by San Juan de Ribera, a towering Counter-Reformation figure who wielded enormous spiritual and temporal power in Spain and beyond. With an impressive if austere Renaissance courtyard-cloister, its main attraction is a small but excellent religious-art museum. Caravaggio, El Greco and local boys José de Ribera and Juan de Juanes are all represented. Most surprising is the manuscript that Thomas More was writing while awaiting his execution in the Tower of London.

The adjacent church has a soberly handsome cloister, some high-quality Renaissance frescoes, and a stuffed caiman, Lepanto, in the anteroom.

Bioparc

Zoo in Western Valencia

Price - adult/child €24/18

Hours - 10am-dusk

Contact - http://www.bioparcvalencia.es

Location - Avenida Pío Baroja 3, Valencia, Spain

This zoo devoted solely to African animals has an educational and conservationist remit and an unusual approach. Though, as always, the confinement in limited spaces of creatures like gorillas raises mixed feelings, the innovative landscaping is certainly a thrill. The absence of obvious fences makes it seem that animals roam free as you wander from savannah to equatorial landscapes. Aardvarks, leopards and hippos draw crowds but most magical is Madagascar, where large-eyed lemurs gambol around your feet among waterfalls and grass.

There are various child-friendly eating points around the zoo.

Seville

Some cities blast you away, others slowly win you over. Seville disarms and seduces you. Its historic centre, lorded over by a colossal Gothic cathedral, is an intoxicating mix of resplendent Mudéjar palaces, baroque churches and winding medieval lanes. Flamenco clubs keep the intimacy and intensity of this centuries-old tradition alive whilst aristocratic mansions recall the city's past as a showcase Moorish capital and, later, a 16th-century metropolis rich on the back of New World trade.

But while history reverberates all around, Seville is as much about the here and now as the past. It's about eating tapas in a crowded bar or seeing out the end of the day over a drink on a buzzing plaza. The sevillanos have long since mastered the art of celebrating and the city's great annual festivals, notably the Semana Santa and Feria de Abril, are among Spain's most heartfelt.

Experiences in Seville

Real Alcázar

Top choice palace in Seville

Price - adult/child €9.50/free

Hours - 9.30am-7pm Apr-Sep, to 5pm Oct-Mar

Contact - http://www.alcazarsevilla.org; 954 50 23 24

Location - Plaza del Triunfo, Seville, Spain

A magnificent marriage of Christian and Mudéjar architecture, Seville's Unesco-listed palace complex is a breathtaking spectacle. The site, which was originally developed as a fort in 913, has been revamped many times over the 11 centuries of its existence, most spectacularly in the 14th century when King Pedro added the sumptuous Palacio de Don Pedro, still today the Alcázar's crown jewel. More recently, the Alcázar featured as a location for the Game of Thrones TV series.

The Alcázar started life in the 10th century as a fort for the Cordoban governors of Seville but it was in the 11th century that it got its first major rebuild. Under the city's Abbadid rulers, the original fort was enlarged and a palace known as Al-Muwarak (the Blessed) was built in what's now the western part of the complex. Subsequently, the 12th-century Almohad rulers added another palace east of this, around what's now the Patio del Crucero. The Christian king Fernando III moved into the Alcázar when he captured Seville in 1248, and several later monarchs used it as their main residence. Fernando's son Alfonso X replaced much of the Almohad palace with a Gothic one and then, between 1364 and 1366, Pedro I created his stunning namesake palace.

Patio del León

Entry to the complex is through the Puerta del León (Lion Gate) on Plaza del Triunfo. Passing through the gateway, which is flanked by crenellated walls, you come to the Patio del León (Lion Patio), which was the garrison yard of the original Al-Muwarak palace. Off to the left before the arches is the Sala de la Justicia (Hall of Justice), with beautiful Mudéjar plasterwork and an artesonado (ceiling of interlaced beams with decorative insertions). This room was built in the 1340s by the Christian King Alfonso XI, who disported here with one of his mistresses, Leonor de Guzmán, reputedly the most beautiful woman in Spain. It leads to the pretty Patio del Yeso, part of the 12th-century Almohad palace reconstructed in the 19th century.

Patio de la Montería

Dominated by the facade of the Palacio de Don Pedro, the Patio de la Monteria owes its name (The Hunting Courtyard) to the fact that hunters would meet here before hunts with King Pedro. Rooms on the western side of the square were part of the Casa de la Contratación (Contracting House), founded in 1503 to control trade with Spain's American colonies. The Salón del Almirante (Admiral's Hall) houses 19th- and 20th-century paintings showing historical events and personages associated with Seville. The room off its northern end has an international collection of beautiful, elaborate fans. The Sala de Audiencias (Chapterhouse) is hung with tapestry representations of the shields of Spanish admirals and Alejo Fernández' celebrated 1530s painting Virgen de los mareantes (Madonna of the Seafarers).

Cuarto Real Alto

The Alcázar is still a royal palace. In 1995 it hosted the wedding feast of Infanta Elena, daughter of King Juan Carlos I, after her marriage in Seville's cathedral. The Cuarto Real Alto (Upper Royal Quarters), the rooms used by the Spanish royal family on their visits to Seville, are open for guided tours (€4.50; half-hourly 10am to 1.30pm; booking required). Highlights of the tours, which are conducted in either Spanish or English, include the 14th-century Salón de Audiencias, still the monarch's reception room, and Pedro I's bedroom, with marvellous Mudéjar tiles and plasterwork.

Palacio de Don Pedro

This palace, also known as the Palacio Mudéjar, is Seville's single most stunning architectural feature.

King Pedro, though at odds with many of his fellow Christians, had a long-standing alliance with the Muslim emir of Granada, Mohammed V, the man responsible for much of the decoration at the Alhambra. So when Pedro decided to build a new palace in the Alcázar in 1364, Mohammed sent many of his top craftsmen. These were joined by others from Seville and Toledo. Their work, drawing on the Islamic traditions of the Almohads and caliphal Córdoba, is a unique synthesis of Iberian Islamic art.

Inscriptions on the palace's façade encapsulate the collaborative nature of the enterprise. While one, in Spanish, announces that the building's creator was the 'highest, noblest and most powerful conqueror Don Pedro, by God's grace King of Castilla and León', another proclaims repeatedly in Arabic that 'there is no conqueror but Allah'.

At the heart of the palace is the sublime Patio de las Doncellas (Patio of the Maidens), surrounded by beautiful arches, plasterwork and tiling. The sunken garden in the centre was uncovered by archaeologists in 2004 from beneath a 16th-century marble covering.

To the north of the patio, the Alcoba Real (Royal Quarters), feature stunningly beautiful ceilings and wonderful plaster- and tilework. Its rear room was probably the monarch's summer bedroom.

Continuing on brings you to the covered Patio de las Muñecas (Patio of the Dolls), the heart of the palace's private quarters, featuring delicate Granada-style decoration; indeed, plasterwork was actually brought here from the Alhambra in the 19th century, when the mezzanine and top gallery were added for Queen Isabel II. The Cuarto del Príncipe (Prince's Suite), to its north, has an elaborate gold ceiling intended to re-create a starlit night sky.

The most spectacular room in the Palacio, and indeed the whole Alcázar, is the Salón de Embajadores (Hall of Ambassadors), south of the Patio de las Muñecas. This was originally Pedro I's throne room, although the fabulous wooden dome of multiple star patterns, symbolising the universe, was added later in 1427. The dome's shape gives the room its alternative name, Sala de la Media Naranja (Hall of the Half Orange).

On the western side of the Salón, the beautiful Arco de Pavones, named after its peacock motifs, leads onto the Salón del Techo de Felipe II, with a Renaissance ceiling (1589–91) and beyond, to the Jardín del Príncipe (Prince's Garden).

Palacio Gótico

Reached via a staircase at the southeastern corner of the Patio de las Doncellas, is Alfonso X's much re-modelled 13th-century Gothic palace. Interest here is centred on the Salones de Carlos V, named after the 16th-century Spanish King Carlos I who was also the Holy Roman Emperor Charles V, and the Salone de los Tapices, a huge vaulted hall with a series of vast tapestries.

Patio del Crucero

Beyond the Salone de los Tapices, the Patio del Crucero was originally the upper storey of a patio from the 12th-century Almohad palace. Initially it consisted only of raised walkways along its four sides and two cross-walkways that met in the middle. Below grew orange trees, whose fruit could be plucked at hand height by the lucky folk strolling along the walkways. The patio's lower level was built over in the 18th century after it suffered earthquake damage.

Gardens & Exit

On the other side of the Salone de los Tapices are the Alcázar's gardens. Formal gardens with pools and fountains sit closest to the palace. From one, the Jardín de la Danza (Garden of the Dance), a passage runs beneath the Salones de Carlos V to the photogenic Baños de Doña María de Padilla (María de Padilla Baths). These are the vaults beneath the Patio del Crucero – originally the patio's lower level – with a grotto that replaced the patio's original pool.

The gardens' most arresting feature is the Galeria de Grutesco, a raised gallery with porticoes fashioned in the 16th century out of an old Muslim-era wall. There is also a fun hedge maze, which will delight children. The gardens to the east, beyond a long wall, are 20th-century creations, but no less heavenly for it.

Catedral & Giralda

Top choice cathedral in Seville

Price - adult/child €9/free, rooftop tours €15

Hours - 11am-3.30pm Mon, to 5pm Tue-Sat, 2.30-6pm Sun

Contact - http://www.catedraldesevilla.es; 954 21 49 71

Location - Plaza del Triunfo, Seville, Spain

Seville's immense cathedral is awe-inspiring in its scale and majesty. The world's largest Gothic cathedral, it was built between 1434 and 1517 over the remains of what had previously been the city's main mosque. Highlights include the Giralda, the mighty bell tower which incorporates the mosque's original minaret, the monumental tomb of Christopher Columbus, and the Capilla Mayor with an astonishing gold altarpiece.

The history of the cathedral goes back to the 15th century but the history of Christian worship on the site dates to the mid-13th century. In 1248, the Castilian King Fernando III captured Seville from its Almohad rulers and transformed their great 12th-century mosque into a church. Some 153 years later, in 1401, the city's ecclesiastical authorities decided to replace the mosque, which had been damaged by an earthquake in 1356, with a spectacular new cathedral: 'Let's construct a church so large future generations will think we were mad', they quipped (or so legend has it).

The result is the staggering cathedral you see today, officially known as the Catedral de Santa María de la Sede. It's one of the world's largest churches and a veritable treasure trove of art with notable works by Zurbarán, Murillo, Goya and others.

Exterior

From close up, the bulky exterior of the cathedral with its Gothic embellishments gives hints of the treasures within. Pause to look at the Puerta del Perdón (now the cathedral's exit) on Calle Alemanes. It's one of the few remaining elements from the original mosque.

Sala del Pabellón

Selected treasures from the cathedral's art collection are exhibited in this room, the first after the ticket office. Much of what's displayed here, as elsewhere in the cathedral, is the work of masters from Seville's 17th-century Golden Age.

Tomb of Christopher Columbus

Once inside the cathedral proper, head right and you'll see the tomb of Christopher Columbus (the Sepolcro de Cristóbal Colón) in front of the Puerta del Principe (Door of the Prince). The monument supposedly contains the remains of the great explorer, but debate continues as to whether the bones are actually his.

Columbus' remains were moved many times after his death (in 1506 in Valladolid, northern Spain), and there are those who claim his real bones lie in Santo Domingo. Certainly his bones spent time in the Dominican Republic after they were shipped to Spanish-controlled Hispaniola from their original resting place, the Monasterio de la Cartuja, in 1537. However, they were later sent to Havana and returned to Seville in 1898.

DNA testing in 2006 proved a match between the bones supposed to be Columbus' and bones known to be from his brother Diego. And while that didn't conclusively solve the mystery, it strongly suggested that the great man really is interred in the tomb that bears his name.

Sacristía de los Cálices

To the right of Columbus' tomb are a series of rooms containing some of the cathedral's greatest masterpieces. First up is the Sacristy of the Chalices, where Francisco de Goya's painting of the Sevillan martyrs, Santas Justa y Rufina (1817), hangs above the altar.

Sacristía Mayor

Next along is this large room with a finely carved stone cupola, created between 1528 and 1547: the arch over its portal has carvings of 16th-century foods. Pedro de Campaña's 1547 El Descendimiento (Descent from the Cross), above the central altar at the southern end, and Francisco de Zurbarán's Santa Teresa, to its right, are two of the cathedral's most precious paintings. Also look out for the Custodia de

Juan de Arfe, a huge 475kg silver monstrance made in the 1580s by Renaissance metalsmith Juan de Arfe.

Sala Capitular

The circular chapterhouse, also called the Cabildo, features a stunning carved dome and a Murillo masterpiece, La inmaculada, set high above the archbishop's throne. The room was built between 1558 and 1592 as a venue for meetings of the cathedral hierarchy.

Capilla Mayor

Even in a church as spectacular as this, the Capilla Mayor (Main Chapel) stands out with its astonishing Gothic retable, reckoned to be the world's largest altarpiece. Begun by Flemish sculptor Pieter Dancart in 1482 and finished by others in 1564, this sea of gilt and polychromed wood holds more than 1000 carved biblical figures. At the centre of the lowest level is a tiny 13th-century silver-plated cedar image of the Virgen de la Sede (Virgin of the See), patron of the cathedral.

West of the Capilla is the Choir into which is incorporated a vast organ.

Southern & Northern Chapels

The chapels along the southern and northern sides of the cathedral hold yet more artistic treasures. Of particular note is the Capilla de San Antonio, at the western end of the northern aisle, housing Murillo's humongous 1656 depiction of the vision of St Anthony of Padua. The painting was victim of a daring art heist in 1874.

Giralda

In the northeastern corner of the cathedral you'll find the entry to the Giralda. The climb to the top involves walking up 35 ramps, built so that the guards could ride up on horseback, and a small flight of stairs at the top. Your reward is sensational rooftop views.

The decorative brick tower, which tops out at 104m, was the minaret of the mosque, constructed between 1184 and 1198 at the height of Almohad power. Its proportions, delicate brick-pattern decoration and colour, which changes with the light, make it perhaps Spain's most perfect Islamic building. The topmost parts – from bell level up – were added in the 16th century, when Spanish Christians were busy 'improving on' surviving Islamic buildings. At the very top is El Giraldillo, a 16th-century bronze weathervane representing 'faith', that has become a symbol of Seville.

Patio de los Naranjos

Outside the cathedral's northern side, this patio was originally the mosque's main courtyard. It's planted with 66 naranjos (orange trees), and has a small Visigothic fountain in the centre. Look out for a stuffed crocodile hanging over the courtyard's doorway – it's a replica of a gift the Sultan of Egypt gave Alfonso X in around 1260.

Hospital de los Venerables Sacerdotes

Top choice museum in Seville

Price - adult/child €8/4, 1st Thu of month to 2pm free

Hours - 10am-2pm Thu-Sat summer, to 6pm Thu-Sat rest of year

Contact - http://www.focus.abengoa.es; 954 56 26 96

Location - Plaza de los Venerables 8, Seville, Spain

This gem of a museum, housed in a former hospice for ageing priests, is one of Seville's most rewarding. The artistic highlight is the Focus-Abengoa Foundation's collection of 17th-century paintings in the Centro Velázquez. It's not a big collection but each work is a masterpiece of its genre – highlights include Diego Velázquez' Santa Rufina, his Inmaculada Concepción, and a sharply vivid portrait of Santa Catalina by Bartolomé Murillo.

Elsewhere, you can admire the Hospital's ornately decorated chapel and delightful patio – a classic composition of porticoes, ceramic tiles and orange trees arranged around a sunken fountain.

Metropol Parasol

Top choice landmark in Seville

Price - €3

Hours - 10am-10.30pm Sun-Thu, to 11pm Fri & Sat

Contact - http://www.metropolsevilla.com; 606 635214

Location - Plaza de la Encarnación, Seville, Spain

Since opening in 2011, the opinion-dividing Metropol Parasol, known locally as las setas (the mushrooms), has become something of a city icon. Designed as a giant sunshade by German architect Jürgen Mayer-Hermann, it's said to be the world's largest wooden structure, and it's certainly a formidable sight with its 30m-high mushroom-like pillars and undulating honeycombed roof. Lifts run up from the basement to the top where you can enjoy killer city views from a winding walkway.

The building, six years in the making, covers a former dead zone in Seville's central district once filled with an ugly car park. Roman ruins discovered during its construction have been cleverly incorporated into its foundations and are now on show at the Museo Antiquarium in the basement below the plaza. The structure also houses the local neighbourhood market, a panoramic cafe and a concert space.

Parque de María Luisa

Park in Seville

Hours - 8am-10pm Sep-Jun, to midnight Jul & Aug

Location - Seville, Spain

A delightful oasis of green, the extensive Parque de María Luisa is a lovely place to escape the noise of the city, with duck ponds, snoozing sevillanos and shady paths snaking under the trees.

If you'd rather continue your cultural exploration than commune with the flowers, the park contains several notable drawcards. Chief among them is Plaza de España, the most extravagant of the building projects completed for the 1929 Exposición Iberoamericana. A vast, brick-and-tile confection, it features fountains, mini-canals, and a series of gaudy tile pictures depicting historical scenes from each Spanish province. You can hire row boats to pootle around the canals for €6 (for 35 minutes).

In the south of the park, the Museo Arqueológico boasts some wonderful Roman sculptures, mosaics and statues – many gathered from the nearby site of Itálica.

Opposite is the Museo de Artes y Costumbres Populares, dedicated to local customs, costumes and traditions.

The park is a great place for children to let off steam and families to bond over a bike ride – four-person quad bikes are available to hire for €12 per half-hour.

Plaza de España

Top choice square in Seville

Location - Avenida de Portugal, Seville, Spain

This bombastic plaza in the Parque de María Luisa was the most grandiose of the building projects completed for the 1929 Exposición Iberoamericana. A huge brick-and-tile confection, it's all very over the top, but it's undeniably impressive with its fountains, mini-canals and Venetian-style bridges. A series of gaudy tile pictures depict maps and historical scenes from each Spanish province.

You can hire row boats to ply the canals for €6 (for 35 minutes).

Museo de Bellas Artes

Museum in Seville

Price - EU citizens/other free/€1.50

Hours - 9am-8pm Tue-Sat, to 3pm Sun mid-Sep–mid-Jun, 9am-3pm Tue-Sun mid-Jun–mid-Sep

Contact - http://www.museodebellasartesdesevilla.es; 955 54 29 42

Location - Plaza del Museo 9, Seville, Spain

Housed in the beautiful former Convento de la Merced, Seville's Fine Arts Museum provides an elegant showcase for a comprehensive collection of Spanish and Sevillan paintings and sculptures. Works date from the 15th to 20th centuries, but the onus is very much on brooding religious paintings from the city's 17th-century Siglo de Oro (Golden Age).

Works are displayed in chronological order, with the Golden Age masterpieces clustered in salas V to X. The most visually arresting room is the convent's former church (sala V), hung with paintings by masters of the Sevillan baroque, above all Murillo. His Inmaculada concepción grande (1650) at the head of the church displays all the curving, twisting movement so central to baroque art. Other artists represented include Pacheco (teacher and father-in-law of Velázquez), Juan de Valdés Leal, Zurbarán (look for his deeply sombre Cristo crucificado, c 1630–35) and sculptor Juan Martínez Montañés.

Also of note is El Greco's portrait of his son Jorge Manuel (c 1600–05), Velázquez's Cabeza de apóstol (1620), and a portrait by Goya in sala XI.

Archivo de Indias

Museum in Seville

Hours - 9.30am-5pm Mon-Sat, 10am-2pm Sun

Contact - 954 50 05 28

Location - Calle Santo Tomás, Seville, Spain

Occupying a former merchant's exchange on the western side of Plaza del Triunfo, the Archivo de Indias provides a fascinating insight into Spain's colonial history. The archive, established in 1785 to house documents and maps relating to Spain's American empire, is vast, boasting 7km of shelves, 43,000 documents, and 80 million pages dating from 1492 to the end of the empire in the 19th century. Most documents are filed away but you can examine some fascinating letters and hand-drawn maps.

Information panels (mostly in Spanish) and a short film tell the full story of the building, itself an impressive sight, and recount the history of the archive. The Renaissance building was extensively refurbished in 2005.

Zaragoza

The ethereal image of the multi-domed Basílica del Pilar reflected in the Río Ebro is a potent symbol of Zaragoza, one of Spain's most underrated regional capitals. There's plenty more fine architecture here too, including a turreted castle with an interior like a mini-Alhambra, and some very creatively displayed underground Roman remains, but Zaragoza's appeal goes well beyond its monuments. Spain's fifth-largest city (and home to over half of Aragón's 1.3 million population), it has one the best tapas and bar scenes in the country and is well stocked with the epoch-defining art of local lad Francisco de Goya, the genius painter who was born a short horse-ride away in 1746.

The historic centre (between the Río Ebro, Calle del Coso and Avenida César Augusto) is refreshingly almost traffic-free, including the vast, 400m-long Plaza del Pilar alongside the famous basilica.

Experiences in Zaragoza

Basílica de Nuestra Señora del Pilar

Top choice church in Zaragoza

Hours - 6.45am-8.30pm Mon-Sat, 6.45am-9.30pm Sun

Contact - http://www.basilicadelpilar.es

Location - Plaza del Pilar, Zaragoza, Spain

Brace yourself for this great baroque cavern of Catholicism. The faithful believe that here on 2 January AD 40 the Virgin Mary appeared to Santiago (St James the Apostle) atop a pillar (pilar) of jasper, and left

191

the pillar behind as testimony of her visit. A chapel was built around the pillar, followed by a series of ever more grandiose churches, culminating in the enormous basilica.

A lift whisks you most of the way up the basilica's northwest tower from where you climb to a superb viewpoint over the domes and city.

Originally designed in 1681 by local architect Felipe Sánchez y Herrera, the basilica was greatly modified in the 18th century by the royal architect Ventura Rodríguez, who added the ultra-baroque Santa Capilla at the east end (housing the legendary pillar), and the flurry of 10 colourfully tiled mini-domes that surround the main dome on the roof.

The famous pillar is topped by a 15th-century Gothic sculpture of the Virgin and child, and is concealed inside an elaborate silver casing which is itself usually three-quarters hidden by the long mantle in which the Virgin image is dressed (except on the 2nd, 12th and 20th of each month). A tiny oval-shaped portion of the pillar is exposed in the passage on the chapel's outer west side and a steady stream of people line up to brush lips with its polished and cracked cheek, which even popes have air-kissed. Parents also line up from 1.30pm to 2pm and 6.30pm to 7.30pm to have their babies blessed next to the Virgin. More than the architecture, these sacred symbols, and the devotion they inspire, are what make this church special.

Hung from the northeast column of the Santa Capilla are two wickedly slim shells that were lobbed at the church during the civil war. They failed to explode. A miracle, said the faithful; typical Czech munitions, said the more cynical.

The basilica's finest artwork is the 16th-century alabaster retablo mayor (main altarpiece) by Damián Forment, facing west in the middle of the basilica. There are also two Goyas: La Adoración del Nombre del Dios, on the ceiling of the coreto (small choir) at the church's far east end, is an early classical piece from 1772; vastly different is Regina Martirum painted above the north aisle in 1780 (in the third cupola from the east). With its blurry impressionistic figures, it was hugely controversial at the time.

Aljafería

Top choice palace in Zaragoza

Price - adult/student & senior/child €5/1/free, Sun free

Hours - 10am-2pm & 4.30-8pm Apr-Oct, 10am-2pm & 4-6.30pm Nov-Mar

Contact - http://www.cortesaragon.es; 976 28 96 83

Location - Calle de los Diputados, Zaragoza, Spain

The Aljafería is Spain's finest Islamic-era edifice outside Andalucía. Built as a fortified palace for Zaragoza's Islamic rulers in the 11th century, it underwent various alterations after 1118 when Zaragoza passed into Christian hands. In the 1490s the Catholic Monarchs, Fernando and Isabel, tacked on their own palace. From the 1590s the Aljafería was developed into more of a fortress than a palace. Twentieth-century restorations brought it back to life, and since 1987 Aragón's regional parliament has been housed here.

Inside the main gate, cross the rather dull introductory courtyard into the Patio de Santa Isabel, once the central courtyard of the Islamic palace. Here you encounter the delicate interwoven arches typical of the geometric mastery of Islamic architecture. Opening off the stunning northern portico is a small, octagonal oratorio (prayer room) with a superb horseshoe-arched doorway leading into its mihrab (prayer niche indicating the direction of Mecca). The finely chiselled floral motifs, Arabic inscriptions from the Quran and a pleasingly simple cupola are fine examples of Islamic art.

Moving upstairs, you pass through rooms of the Palacio Cristiano Medieval, created mostly by Aragonese monarchs in the 14th century, followed by the Palacio de los Reyes Católicos (Catholic Monarchs' Palace) which, as though by way of riposte to the Islamic finery beneath it, contains some exquisite Mudéjar coffered ceilings, especially in the lavish Salón del Trono (Throne Room).

Spanish-language tours take place several times a day, and there are two daily tours each in English and French in July and August. The palace is often closed Thursday, Friday morning or Sunday afternoon in non-peak times.

Museo Goya – Colección Ibercaja

Top choice museum in Zaragoza

Price - adult/senior or child €4/free, audioguide or tablet €2

Hours - 10am-8pm Mon-Sat, 10am-2pm Sun Apr-Oct, 10am-2pm & 4pm-8pm Mon-Sat, 10am-2pm Sun Nov-Mar

Contact - http://museogoya.ibercaja.es; 976 39 73 87

Location - Calle de Espoz y Mina 23, Zaragoza, Spain

Apart from Madrid's Museo del Prado, this exceedingly well laid-out museum contains arguably the best exposé of the work of one of Spain's most revered artists. Each of the three floors has a different focus, the second floor being the one that exhibits Goya's own work. Four complete sets of his prints are included, most notably the groundbreaking, sometimes grotesque Desastres de la Guerra (Disasters of War), a bitter attack on the cruelty and folly of war.

Also here are Goya's first self-portrait (1775) and his well-known portraits of king Carlos IV and queen María Luisa. The first floor amasses some of the art that influenced Goya. The top floor investigates Goya's enormous influence by tracking through the work of his imitators and followers.

Museo del Teatro de Caesaraugusta

Top choice museum in Zaragoza

Price - adult/student/senior & child €4/3/free

Hours - 10am-2pm & 5-9pm Tue-Sat, 10am-2.30pm Sun

Contact - http://www.zaragozaturismo.es; 976 72 60 75

Location - Calle de San Jorge 12, Zaragoza, Spain

The finest in Zaragoza's quartet of Roman museums was discovered during excavation of a building site in 1972. Great efforts, including an entertaining 15-minute audiovisual, have been made to help visitors visualise the splendour of this theatre that accommodated 6000 spectators on more than 30 rows of seating. The theatre is visible from the surrounding streets and is protected by a huge polycarbonate roof, 25m above ground, that is set at the height of the top of the original building.

The adjoining museum goes into interesting detail about Roman drama, the history of the theatre and the actors and audiences who frequented it, and what happened on its site in post-Roman times.

La Seo

Top choice cathedral in Zaragoza

Price - adult/senior/child €4/3/free

Hours - 10am-6.30pm & 7.45-9pm Mon-Thu, 10am-6.30pm Fri, 10am-noon, 3-6.30pm & 7.45-9pm Sat & Sun mid-Jun–mid-Oct, 10am-2pm & 4-6.30pm mid-Oct–mid-Jun

Contact - http://www.zaragozaturismo.es; 976 29 12 31

Location - Plaza de la Seo, Zaragoza, Spain

Dominating the eastern end of Plaza del Pilar, La Seo is Zaragoza's finest work of Christian architecture, built between the 12th and 17th centuries and displaying a fabulous spread of styles from Romanesque to baroque. It stands on the site of Islamic Zaragoza's main mosque (which itself stood upon the temple of the Roman forum). The admission Price includes La Seo's Museo de Tapices, a collection of Flemish and French tapestries considered the best of its kind in the world.

The cathedral's northeast external wall is a Mudéjar masterpiece, deploying classic brickwork and colourful ceramic decoration in complex geometric patterns. Inside, beautiful fan vaulting adorns the ceiling while the chapels, framed by encrusted stonework, ring the changes from the eerie solemnity of the Capilla de San Marcos to the golden baroque baldachin of the Capilla del Santo Cristo. The exquisite 15th-century alabaster high altarpiece is well worth scrutiny too.

Museo de Zaragoza

Museum in Zaragoza

Hours - 10am-2pm & 5-8pm Tue-Sat, 10am-2pm Sun

Contact - http://www.museodezaragoza.es

Location - Plaza de los Sitios 6, Zaragoza, Spain

Devoted to archaeology and fine arts, the city museum displays artefacts from prehistoric to Islamic times, with some exceptional mosaics from Roman Caesaraugusta. The upper floor contains 19 paintings by Goya and more than two dozen of his prints. It's 400m south of the Teatro Romano.

The Goyas are mostly early works but there are a few mature works such as the outstanding portraits of the Duque de San Carlos and Fernando VII. The portraits of Carlos IV and María Luisa de Parma are copies from Goya's workshop of originals that hang in the Museo de Goya.

Alma Mater Museum

Museum in Zaragoza

Price - €3

Hours - 10am-8pm Tue-Sat, 10am-2pm Sun

Contact - http://www.almamatermuseum.com; 976 39 94 88

Location - Plaza de la Seo 5, Zaragoza, Spain

Church museums can sometimes be boring emporiums of anonymous sacred art, but not this one. Slick multimedia exhibits set an arty tone which is continued as you navigate through a skilfully laid-out trajectory that takes in the older elements of the building (a former royal and episcopal palace), learning about Roman forums, the venerated Virgen del Pilar and Aragonese history (especially church history). The top floor is a Renaissance feast with paintings by the two local Francsicos, Goya and Bayeu.

Museo Origami

Museum in Zaragoza

Price - adult/student & senior €3/2

Hours - 10am-2pm & 5-9pm Tue-Sat, 10am-2.30pm Sun

Contact - http://www.emoz.es; 876 03 45 69

Location - Centro de Historias, Plaza San Agustín 2, Zaragoza, Spain

This museum devoted to the art of folding paper has six galleries of permanent and temporary exhibitions of a staggeringly high standard. It attracts worldwide interest from origami aficionados. If you're not very familiar with the art, you will probably be amazed by what you see.

You can also take hour-long origami classes (€6); check the website for more information and to learn about Zaragoza's fascinating historical connection with origami (dating back to the 1940s).

Málaga

Málaga is a world apart from the adjoining Costa del Sol: a historic and culturally rich provincial capital which has long lived in the shadow of the iconic Andalucian cities of Granada, Córdoba and Seville. Yet, it has rapidly emerged as the province's city of culture with its so-called 'mile of art' being compared to Madrid, and its dynamism and fine dining to Barcelona.

The tastefully restored historic centre is a delight: its Gothic cathedral is surrounded by narrow pedestrian streets flanked by traditional and modern bars, and shops that range from idiosyncratic and family owned, to urban-chic and contemporary. Cast your eyes up to enjoy a skyline that reflects the city's eclectic character; church spires jostle for space with russet-red tiled roofs and lofty apartment buildings while, like a grand old dame, the 11th-century Gibralfaro castle sits grandly aloft and provides the best view of all.

The former rundown port has also been grandly rebuilt and cruise-line passengers are now boosting the city's coffers and contributing to the overall increase in tourism to the city.

Experiences in Málaga

Catedral de Málaga

Top choice cathedral in Málaga

Price - cathedral & museum €5, tower €6

Hours - 10am-6pm Mon-Sat

Contact - http://www.malagaturismo.com; 952 21 59 17

Location - Calle Molina Lario, Málaga, Spain

Málaga's cathedral was started in the 16th century on the site of the former mosque. Of the mosque, only the Patio de los Naranjos survives, a small courtyard of fragrant orange trees.

Inside, the fabulous domed ceiling soars 40m into the air, while the vast colonnaded nave houses an enormous cedar-wood choir. Aisles give access to 15 chapels with gorgeous 18th-century retables and religious art. Climb the tower (200 steps) to enjoy stunning panoramic views of the city skyline and coast.

Building the cathedral was an epic project that took some 200 years. Such was the project's cost that by 1782 it was decided that work would stop. One of the two bell towers was left incomplete, hence the cathedral's well-worn nickname, La Manquita (the one-armed lady). The cathedral's museum displays a collection of religious items covering a period of 500 years.

Alcazaba

Top choice castle in Málaga

Price - €2.20, incl Castillo de Gibralfaro €3.40

Hours - 9.30am-8pm Tue-Sun

Contact - http://www.malagaturismo.com; 630 932987

Location - Calle Alcazabilla, Málaga, Spain

No time to visit Granada's Alhambra? Then Málaga's Alcazaba can provide a taster. The entrance is next to the Roman amphitheatre, from where a meandering path climbs amid lush greenery: crimson bougainvillea, lofty palms, fragrant jasmine bushes and rows of orange trees. Extensively restored, this palace-fortress dates from the 11th-century Moorish period; the caliphal horseshoe arches, courtyards and bubbling fountains are evocative of this influential period in Málaga's history.

Don't miss the small archaeological museum located within the former servants' quarters of the Nazari palace, with its exhibits of Moorish ceramics and pottery.

Museo Picasso Málaga

Top choice museum in Málaga

Price - €7, incl temporary exhibition €10

Hours - 10am-8pm Jul-Aug, to 7pm Mar-Jun & Sep-Oct, to 6pm Nov-Feb

Contact - http://www.museopicassomalaga.org; 902 443377

Location - Calle San Agustín 8, Málaga, Spain

The Museo Picasso has an enviable collection of 204 works, 155 donated and 49 loaned to the museum by Christine Ruiz-Picasso (wife of Paul, Picasso's eldest son) and Bernard Ruiz-Picasso (his grandson), and includes some wonderful paintings of the family, including the heartfelt Paulo con gorro blanco (Paulo with a white cap), a portrait of Picasso's eldest son painted in the 1920s.

Don't miss the Phoenician, Roman, Islamic and Renaissance archaeological remains in the museum's basement, discovered during construction works.

There are also excellent year-round temporary exhibitions.

Centre Pompidou Málaga

Top choice museum in Málaga

Price - €7, incl temporary exhibition €9

Hours - 9.30am-8pm Wed-Mon

Contact - http://www.centrepompidou.es; 951 92 62 00

Location - Pasaje Doctor Carrillo Casaux, Muelle Uno, Málaga, Spain

Opened in 2015 in the port, this offshoot of the Paris Pompidou Centre is housed in a low-slung modern building crowned by a playful multicoloured cube. The permanent exhibition includes the extraordinary Ghost, by Kader Attia, depicting rows of Muslim women bowed in prayer and created from domestic aluminium foil, plus works by such modern masters as Frida Kahlo, Francis Bacon and Antoni Tàpies. There are also audiovisual installations, talking 'heads' and temporary exhibitions.

The museum is contracted to be here for five years at an annual cost of a cool €1 million.

Castillo de Gibralfaro

Castle in Málaga

Price - €2.20, incl Alcazaba €3.40

Hours - 9am-9pm Apr-Sep

Contact - http://www.malagaturismo.com; 952 22 72 30

Location - Camino Gibralfaro; Málaga, Spain

One remnant of Málaga's Islamic past is the craggy ramparts of the Castillo de Gibralfaro, spectacularly located high on the hill overlooking the city. Built by Abd ar-Rahman I, the 8th-century Cordoban emir, and later rebuilt in the 14th century when Málaga was the main port for the emirate of Granada, the castle originally acted as a lighthouse and military barracks.

Nothing much is original in the castle's interior, but the airy walkway around the ramparts affords the best views over Málaga.

There is also a military museum, which includes a small scale model of the entire castle complex and the lower residence, the Alcazaba.

The best way to reach the castle on foot is via the scenic Paseo Don Juan de Temboury, to the south of the Alcazaba. From here a path winds pleasantly (and steeply) through lushly gardened terraces with viewpoints over the city. Alternatively, you can drive up the Camino de Gibralfaro or take bus 35 from Avenida de Cervantes.

Mercado Atarazanas

Market in Málaga

Location - Calle Atarazanas, Málaga, Spain

North of the city's main artery, the Alameda Principal, you'll find this striking 19th-century iron-clad building incorporating the original Moorish gate that once connected the city with the port. The magnificent stained-glass window depicts historical highlights of the city.

The daily market here is pleasantly noisy and animated. Choose from swaying legs of ham and rolls of sausages or cheese, fish and endless varieties of olives. The fruit and veg stalls are the most colourful, selling everything that is in season, ranging from big misshapen tomatoes, sliced and served with olive oil, chopped garlic and rough salt, to large purple onions, mild-flavoured and sweet.

Museo Ruso de Málaga

Museum in Málaga

Price - adult/child €8/free

Hours - 11am-10pm Tue-Sun

Contact - http://www.coleccionmuseoruso.es; 951 92 61 50

Location - Avenida de Sor Teresa Plat 15, Málaga, Spain

This offshoot of the Russian State Museum in St Petersburg opened in 2015 in a former 1920s tobacco factory. It is dedicated to Russian art from the 16th to 20th centuries, featuring works by Ilya Repin, Wassily Kandinsky and Vladimir Tatlin, among others. From Málaga Centre Alameda Principal, take bus 3, 15 or 16 and get off at Avenida La Paloma (€1.35, 10 minutes).

This museum is essentially a 'pop-up' with a 10-year contract to remain in Málaga.

MAUS

Area in Málaga

Location - Málaga, Spain

The antithesis of Málaga's prestigious world-class art museums is refreshingly down-to-earth MUES (Málaga Arte Urbano en el Soho) a grassroots movement originally born from an influx of street artists to the area. The result is a total transformation of the formerly rundown district between the city centre and the port (now called Soho), with edgy contemporary murals, several stories high, as well as arty cafes, ethnic restaurants and street markets.

Murcia

Officially twinned with Miami, Murcia is the antithesis of the city of vice; it's a laid-back provincial capital that comes alive during the weekend paseo (stroll). Bypassed by most tourists and treated as a country cousin by many Spaniards, the city nevertheless more than merits a visit. The city is blessed with many excellent restaurants that use local market produce.

Experiences in Murcia

Real Casino de Murcia

Top choice historic building in Murcia

Price - adult/child €5/3

Hours - 10.30am-7pm

Contact - http://www.casinodemurcia.com

Location - Calle de la Trapería 18, Murcia, Spain

Murcia's resplendent casino first opened as a gentlemen's club in 1847. Painstakingly restored to its original glory, the building is a fabulous combination of historical design and opulence, providing an evocative glimpse of bygone aristocratic grandeur. Beyond the decorative facade are a dazzling Moorish-style patio; a classic English-style library with

20,000 books; a magnificent ballroom with glittering chandeliers; and a compelling tocador (ladies' powder room) with a ceiling fresco of cherubs, angels and an alarming winged woman in flames.

There is also the neoclassical patio pompeyano and the classic wood-panelled sala de billar (billiards room).

Catedral de Santa María

Cathedral in Murcia

Hours - 7am-1pm & 5-8pm Sep-Jun, 7am-1pm & 6.30-8pm Jul & Aug

Contact - 968 35 87 49

Location - Plaza del Cardenal Belluga, Murcia, Spain

Murcia's cathedral was built in 1394 on the site of a mosque. The initial Gothic architecture was given a playful baroque facelift in 1748, with a stunning facade facing on to the plaza. The 15th-century Capilla de los Vélez is a highlight; the chapel's flutes and curls resemble icing. The Museo Catedralicio displays religious artefacts, but is most noteworthy for the excavations on display.

Museo de Bellas Artes

Gallery in Murcia

Hours - 10am-2pm & 5-8pm Tue-Fri, 11am-2pm & 5-8pm Sat, 11am-2pm Sun, mornings only Jul & Aug

Contact - http://www.museosdemurcia.com; 968 23 93 46

Location - Calle del Obispo Frutos 12, Murcia, Spain

An inviting, light gallery devoted to Spanish artists. Much is mediocre, but the 2nd-floor Siglo de Oro gallery has two fabulous Murillos – a Crucifixion and an Ecce Homo – and a powerful chiaroscuro San Jerónimo by Ribera. Look out for the faintest shadow of his tame lion. The 3rd floor holds temporary exhibitions.

Museo Catedralicio

Museum in Murcia

Price - adult/child €3/2

Hours - 10am-5pm Tue-Sat, 10am-1pm Sun Jul-Sep, 10am-1pm & 4-7pm Tue-Sat, 10am-1pm Sun Oct-Jun

Location - Plaza de la Cruz 1, Murcia, Spain

The cathedral museum displays religious artefacts but is most striking for the excavations on display: the remains of an 11th-century Moorish dwelling and of a small mezquita (mosque), evocatively visible below a sturdy glass walkway. Guided visits include an ascent of the belltower.

Jardín Floridablanca

Park in Murcia

The classic, small but beautiful Jardín Floridablanca has several magnificent banyan trees distinctive for their massive spread of thick woody roots, as well as jacarandas, cypress trees, palms, rose bushes and shady benches, plenty of them, for contemplating the view.

Palma de Mallorca

Palma is a stunner. Rising in honey-coloured stone from the broad waters of the Badia de Palma, this enduring city dates back to the 13th-century Christian reconquest of the island, and to the Moors, Romans and Talayotic people before that. A richly studded diadem of historical sites, Palma also shelters a seemingly endless array of galleries, restaurants, craft studios and bars – it's without doubt Mallorca's greatest treasure. Wander in any direction from the awe-inspiring Gothic Catedral at its geographic and historical heart and you'll find bent medieval streets lined with aristocratic townhouses, looming baroque churches, teeming public squares, vibrant bohemian neighbourhoods and markets overflowing with all the bounty of the island. You could spend weeks in this city alone, and still uncover fresh joys every day.

Experiences in Palma de Mallorca

Palau de l'Almudaina

Top choice palace in Palma de Mallorca

Price - adult/child €7/4, audio guide/guided tour €3/4

Hours - 10am-8pm Apr-Sep, to 6pm Oct-Mar

Contact - http://www.patrimonionacional.es

Location - Carrer del Palau Reial, Palma de Mallorca, Spain

Originally an Islamic fort, this mighty construction opposite the cathedral was converted into a residence for the Mallorcan monarchs at the end of the 13th century. The King of Spain resides here still, at least symbolically. The royal family are rarely in residence, except for the occasional ceremony, as they prefer to spend summer in the Palau Marivent (in Cala Major). At other times you can wander through a series of cavernous stone-walled rooms that have been lavishly decorated.

The Romans are said to have built a castrum (fort) here, possibly on the site of a prehistoric settlement. The Wālis (Governors) of Muslim Mallorca altered and expanded the Roman original to build their own alcázar (fort), before Jaume I and his successors modified it to such an extent that little of the Muslim version remains.

The first narrow room you enter has a black-and-white ceiling, symbolising the extremes of night and day, darkness and light. You then enter a series of three grand rooms. Notice the bricked-in Gothic arches cut off in the middle. Originally these three rooms were double their present height and formed one single great hall added to the original Arab fort and known as the Saló del Tinell (from an Italian word, tinello, meaning 'place where one eats'): this was once a giant banqueting and ceremonial hall. The rooms are graced by period furniture, tapestries and other curios. The following six bare rooms and terrace belonged to the original Arab citadel.

In the main courtyard, Patio de Armas, troops would line up for an inspection and parade before heading out into the city. The lion fountain in its centre is one of the palace's rare Arab remnants. Up the grand Royal Staircase are the royal apartments, a succession of lavishly appointed rooms (look up to the beautiful coffered timber artesonado ceilings), whose centrepiece is the Saló Gòtic, the upper half of the former Saló del Tinell; here you can see where those Gothic arches wind up. Next door to the apartments is the royal Capella de Sant'Anna, a Gothic chapel whose entrance is a very rare Mallorcan example of late Romanesque in rose and white marble.

After the death of Jaume III in 1349, no king lived here permanently again.

In the shadow of the Almudaina's walls, along Avinguda d'Antoni Maura, is S'Hort del Rei (the King's Garden).

Palau March

Top choice museum in Palma de Mallorca

Price - adult/child €4.50/free

Hours - 10am-6.30pm Mon-Fri Apr-Oct, to 2pm Nov-Mar, to 2pm Sat year-round

Contact - http://www.fundacionbmarch.es; 971 71 11 22

Location - Carrer del Palau Reial 18, Palma de Mallorca, Spain

This house, palatial by any definition, was one of several residences of the phenomenally wealthy March family. Sculptures by 20th-century greats including Henry Moore, Auguste Rodin, Barbara Hepworth and Eduardo Chillida grace the outdoor terrace. Within lie many more artistic treasures from such luminaries of Spanish art as Salvador Dalí and Barcelona's Josep Maria Sert and Xavier Corberó. Not to be missed are the meticulously crafted figures of an 18th-century Neapolitan belén (nativity scene).

Entry is through an outdoor terrace display of modern sculptural works, of which centre stage is taken by Corberó's enormous Orgue del Mar (1973), or perhaps Rodin's Torse de l'Homme qui Tombe (1882).

Inside, more than 20 paintings by Dalí around the themes 'Alchemy and Eternity' catch the eye, as does the belén's 1000-plus detailed figures, from angels to kings, shepherds, farm animals and market scenes, making up a unique representation of Christ's birth.

Upstairs, the artist Josep Maria Sert (1874–1945) painted the main vault and music room ceiling. The vault is divided into four parts, the first three representing three virtues (audacity, reason and inspiration) and the last the embodiment of those qualities in the form of Sert's patron, Juan March (1917–98). One of the rooms hosts an intriguing display of maps of the Mediterranean, produced by Mallorcan cartographers in medieval and early modern times.

Catedral de Mallorca

Top choice cathedral in Palma de Mallorca

Price - adult/child €7/free

Hours - 10am-6.15pm Mon-Fri Jun-Sep, to 5.15pm Apr, May & Oct, to 3.15pm Nov-Mar, 10am-2.15pm Sat year-round

Contact - http://www.catedraldemallorca.org

Location - Carrer del Palau Reial 9, Palma de Mallorca, Spain

Palma's vast cathedral ('La Seu' in Catalan) is the city's major architectural landmark. Aside from its sheer scale and undoubted beauty, its stunning interior features, designed by Antoni Gaudí and renowned contemporary artist Miquel Barceló, make this unlike any cathedral elsewhere in the world. The awesome structure is predominantly Gothic, apart from the main facade, which is startling, quite beautiful and completely mongrel.

The Catedral occupies the site of what was the central mosque of Medina Mayurka, capital of Muslim Mallorca for three centuries. Although Jaume I and his marauding men forced their way into the city in 1229, work on the Catedral – one of Europe's largest – did not begin until 1300. Rather, the mosque was used in the interim as a church and dedicated to the Virgin Mary. Work wasn't completed until 1601.

The original was a Renaissance cherry on the Gothic cake, but an earthquake in 1851 (which caused considerable panic but no loss of life) severely damaged it. Rather than mend the original, it was decided to add some neo-Gothic flavour. With its interlaced flying buttresses on each flank and soaring pinnacles, it's a masterful example of the style. The result is a hybrid of the Renaissance original (in particular the main doorway) and an inevitably artificial-feeling, 19th-century pseudo-Gothic monumentalism.

Mass times vary, but one always takes place at 9am.

Es Baluard

Top choice gallery in Palma de Mallorca

Price - adult/temporary exhibitions/child €6/4/free

Hours - 10am-8pm Tue-Sat, to 3pm Sun

Contact - http://www.esbaluard.org; 971 90 82 00

Location - Plaça de Porta de Santa Catalina 10, Palma de Mallorca, Spain

Built with flair and innovation into the shell of the Renaissance-era seaward walls, this contemporary art gallery is one of the finest on the island. Its temporary exhibitions are worth viewing, but the permanent collection – works by Miró, Barceló and Picasso – give the gallery its cachet. Entry on Fridays is by donation, and anyone turning up on a bike, on any day, is charged just €2.

The 21st-century concrete complex is cleverly built among the fortifications, including the partly restored remains of an 11th-century Muslim-era tower (on your right as you arrive from Carrer de Sant Pere). Inside, the ground floor houses the core of the permanent exhibition, starting with a section on Mallorcan landscapes by local artists and others from abroad; the big names here include Valencia's Joaquín Sorolla, Mallorca's own Miquel Barceló and the Catalan Modernista artist Santiago Rusiñol.

Also on the ground floor and part of the permanent collection is a room devoted to the works of Joan Miró, while on the top floor is an intriguing collection of ceramics by Pablo Picasso; after viewing the latter, step out onto the ramparts for fine views. In sum, it's an impressive rather than extraordinary collection that's well worth a couple of hours of your time.

Museu Fundación Juan March

Top choice gallery in Palma de Mallorca

Hours - 10am-6.30pm Mon-Fri, 10.30am-2pm Sat

Contact - http://www.march.es; 91 435 42 40

Location - Carrer de Sant Miquel 11, Palma de Mallorca, Spain

The 17th-century Can Gallard del Canya, a 17th-century mansion overlaid with minor Modernist touches, now houses a small but significant collection of painting and sculpture. The permanent exhibits – some 80 pieces held by the Fundación Juan March – constitute a veritable who's who of contemporary Spanish art, including Miró,

Picasso, fellow cubist Juan Gris, Dalí, and the sculptors Eduardo Chillida and Julio González.

After starting with the big names, the collection skips through various movements in Spanish art, such as that inspired in Barcelona by the Dau al Set review (1948–53) and led by Antoni Tàpies. Meanwhile, in Valencia, Eusebio Sempere and Andreu Alfaro were leading the way down abstract paths. Sempere's Las Cuatro Estaciones (1980) reflects the four seasons in subtle changes of colour in a series of four panels with interlocking shapes made of fine lines. Other names to watch for are Manuel Millares, Fernando Zóbel and Miquel Barceló, who is represented by works including his large-format La Flaque (The Pond; 1989).

Castell de Bellver

Castle in Palma de Mallorca

Price - adult/child €4/2, free Sun

Hours - 8.30am-1pm Mon, to 8pm Tue-Sat, 10am-8pm Sun

Contact - http://castelldebellver.palma.cat; 971 73 50 65

Location - Carrer de Camilo José Cela, Palma de Mallorca, Spain

Straddling a wooded hillside, the Castell de Bellver is a 14th-century circular castle (with a unique round tower), the only one of its kind in Spain. Jaume II ordered it built atop a hill known as Puig de Sa Mesquida in 1300 and it was largely completed within 10 years. Perhaps the highlight of any visit is the spectacular views over the woods to Palma, the Badia de Palma and out to sea.

The castle was conceived above all as a royal residence but seems to have been a white elephant, as only King Sanç (in 1314) and Aragón's Joan I (in 1395) moved in for any amount of time. In 1717 it became a military prison, and was subsequently used in both the Napoleonic and Spanish Civil Wars. Climb to the roof and check out the prisoners' graffiti, etched into the stonework.

The ground-floor Museu d'Història de la Ciutat (City History Museum) traces the development of the city from the prehistoric Talayotic civilisation to the present day. As well as Roman and Arabian ceramics there are explanatory panels, the classical statues of the Despuig Collection and other artefacts. Upstairs you can visit a series of largely empty chambers, including the one-time kitchen.

About the nearest you can get to the castle by bus (3, 46 or 50) is Plaça de Gomila, from where you'll have to hoof it about 15 minutes (1km) up a steep hill. Instead, combine it with the Palma City Sightseeing open-top bus, which climbs to the castle as part of its circuit of the city.

Basílica de Sant Francesc

Church in Palma de Mallorca

Price - 6-venue Spiritual Mallorca ticket €5

Hours - 10am-2pm & 3-6pm Mon-Sat

Location - Plaça de Sant Francesc 7, Palma de Mallorca, Spain

One of Palma's oldest churches, the Franciscan Basílica de Sant Francesc was begun in 1281 in Gothic style, while the baroque facade, with its carved postal and rose window, was completed in 1700. In the splendid Gothic cloister – a two-tiered, trapezoid affair – the elegant columns indicate it was some time in the making. Inside, the high vaulted roof is classic Gothic, while the glittering high altar is a baroque lollipop, albeit in need of a polish.

In the first chapel (dedicated to Nostra Senyora de la Consolació) on the left in the apse is the church's pride and joy, the tomb of the 13th-century scholar and mystic Ramon Llull. Also a fervid evangelist and the inventor of literary Catalan, Llull lays fair claim to the title of Mallorca's favourite son (apart perhaps from tennis genius Rafael Nadal). His alabaster tomb is high up on the right – drop a few coins in the slot for the campaign to have him canonised (he has only made it to beatification). Check out the Capilla de los Santos Mártires Gorkomienses, on the right side of the apse. In 1572, 19 Catholics, 11 of them Franciscans, were martyred in Holland. In this much-faded portrayal of the event, you can see them being hanged, disembowelled, having their noses cut off and more.

Museu de sa Jugueta

Museum in Palma de Mallorca

Price - adult/child €3.50/2.50

Hours - 9.30am-5pm Tue & Wed, to 12.30pm Thu-Sat

Contact - http://www.museudesajugueta.es; 654 650780

Location - Carrer de la Campana 7, Palma de Mallorca, Spain

The 3000 cars, planes, dolls, robots and other toys on display here represent the tip of a collection of more than 7000 pieces, acquired steadily by a passionate collector from Barcelona. Adjoining is a smart little bar-restaurant (three courses for €13) that not only caters to kids, but turns into a creative play space between 5pm and 8pm in the evening.

Las Palmas de Gran Canaria

Las Palmas has a mainland-Spain feel, spiced up with an eclectic mix of other cultures, including African, Chinese and Indian, plus the presence of container-ship crews, and the flotsam and jetsam that tend to drift around port cities. It's an intriguing place, with the sunny languor and energy you would normally associate with the Mediterranean or north Africa. The hooting taxis, bustling shopping districts, chatty bars and thriving port all give off the energy of this city, which is Spain's ninth-largest.

Experiences in Las Palmas de Gran Canaria

Casa-Museo de Colón

Museum in Las Palmas de Gran Canaria

Price - adult/child €4/free

Hours - 10am-6pm Mon-Sat, to 3pm Sun

Contact - http://www.casadecolon.com; 928 31 23 73

Location - Calle Colón 1, Las Palmas de Gran Canaria, Spain

This fascinating museum documents Columbus' voyages and features exhibits on the Canary Islands' historical role as a staging post for transatlantic shipping. Don't miss the model galleon on the ground floor, which particularly impresses children. The crucifix is said to have come from Columbus' ship. Upstairs there is an art gallery and some models of

Las Palmas past and present. Travel geeks will love rooms five and six, which contain historical maps largely from the early 16th century.

The building is a superb example of Canarian architecture, built around two balconied patios, complete with fountains, palm trees and parrots. The exterior is a work of art itself, with some showy plateresque (silversmith-like) elements, combined with traditional heavy wooden balconies.

Although called Columbus' House (it's possible he stopped here in 1492), most of what you see dates from the time this building was the opulent residence of Las Palmas' early governors.

Playa de las Canteras

Top choice beach in Las Palmas de Gran Canaria

The fine 3km stretch of yellow sand is magnificent, and considered by many to be one of the world's best city beaches. There's an attractive seaside promenade – the Paseo de las Canteras – which allows walkers, cyclists and joggers to cover the entire length of the beach, free from traffic. Perhaps the most marvellous part, though, is the reef, known as La Barra, which in low tide turns the waters of Las Canteras into a giant salty swimming pool that's perfect for snorkelling.

Further south, the restaurants and hotels peter out and the waves become a little bigger. It is here, near the auditorium in an area known as La Cicer, that surfers congregate in the water and footballers take to the sand.

Museo Elder de la Ciencia y la Tecnología

Museum in Las Palmas de Gran Canaria

Price - adult/child €5/3.50, incl 3D film €8.50/€7

Hours - 10am-8pm Tue-Sun

Contact - http://www.museoelder.org

Location - Parque Santa Catalina, Las Palmas de Gran Canaria, Spain

This 21st-century museum is full of things that whirr, clank and hum. In a revamped dockside warehouse in Parque Santa Catalina, it's a great space to spend a few hours. You can pilot a supersonic fighter plane, see how rockets send satellites into orbit or ride the Robocoaster where a robotic arm whizzes you through a series of programmable manoeuvres. Children will be rapt – the space pod and Van de Graaff generator are particularly popular.

There is also a small theatre showing a regularly changing programme of 3D films.

Catedral de Santa Ana & Museo Diocesano de Arte Sacro

Cathedral in Las Palmas de Gran Canaria

Price - adult/child €3/free

Hours - 10am-5pm Mon-Fri, to 2pm Sun

Contact - 928 33 14 30

Location - Calle Obispo Codina 13, Las Palmas de Gran Canaria, Spain

The spiritual heart of the city, this brooding, grey cathedral was begun in the early 15th century, soon after the Spanish conquest, but took 350 years to complete. The neoclassical facade contrasts with the interior, which is a fine example of what some art historians have named Atlantic Gothic, with lofty columns that seem to mimic the palm trees outside. There are also several paintings by Juan de Miranda, the islands' most-respected 18th-century artist.

The ticket also includes entrance to the sacred art museum, set on two levels around the Patio de los Naranjos. It contains a fairly standard collection of religious art and memorabilia, including centuries-old manuscripts, wooden sculptures and other ornaments, but the setting is lovely – and fragrant, with the scent of orange blossom in springtime.

Once you've explored within, take the lift (admission €1.50) to the top of the bell tower for a stunning wide-angle view of the surrounding city and its coast.

Centro Atlántico de Arte Moderno

244

Gallery in Las Palmas de Gran Canaria

Price - adult/child €5/free

Hours - 10am-9pm Tue-Sat, to 2pm Sun

Contact - http://www.caam.net; 928 31 18 00

Location - Calle Balcones 11, Las Palmas de Gran Canaria, Spain

The city's main modern art museum is housed in a tastefully rejuvenated 18th-century building. There are no permanent collections but the galleries, flooded with natural light, host some superb temporary exhibitions. There are two satellite galleries also featuring rotating exhibitions: CAAM San Antonio Abad, near Casa de Colon, and the San Martín Centro de Cultura Contemporánea, based in a former hospital. A combined ticket to enter all three is €8 per adult.

Pueblo Canario

Area in Las Palmas de Gran Canaria

Hours - 10am-8pm Tue-Sat, to 2.30pm Sun

Location - Las Palmas de Gran Canaria, Spain

Designed by artist Néstor Martín Fernández de la Torre and built by his brother Miguel, this mock Canarian village borders the gardens of the Parque Doramas. It's a little unloved and the restaurant keeps sporadic hours, but it's worth a visit on Sunday mornings, when traditional folk music is played here at 11.30am. The pueblo is located on the south side of the Parque Doramas, accessed from Calle León y Castillo.

Casa-Museo de Pérez Galdós

Museum in Las Palmas de Gran Canaria

Price - adult/child €3/free

Hours - 10am-6pm Tue-Fri, to 2pm Sat & Sun

Contact - http://www.casamuseoperezgaldos.com

Location - Calle Cano 6, Las Palmas de Gran Canaria, Spain

In 1843 the Canary Islands' most famous writer, Benito Pérez Galdós, was born in this house in the heart of old Las Palmas. He spent the first 19 years of his life here before moving on to Madrid and literary greatness. Guided tours (in English and Spanish) explore the upstairs rooms, with a reconstruction of the author's study and various personal effects transported from his mainland Spain home following his death.

Museo Canario

Museum in Las Palmas de Gran Canaria

Price - adult/child €4/free

Hours - 10am-8pm Mon-Fri, to 2pm Sat & Sun

Contact - http://www.elmuseocanario.com; 928 33 68 00

Location - Calle Dr Verneau 2, Las Palmas de Gran Canaria, Spain

This slightly old fashioned yet still fascinating museum chronicles Gran Canaria's preconquest history. It claims the heady boast of having the largest collection of Cro-Magnon skulls in the world. There are also several mummies, plus a collection of pottery and other Guanche implements from across the island. The gift shop stocks some excellent children's educational material.

Bilbao

Staggering architecture, a venerable dining scene and stunning landscapes just outside the city centre: Bilbao is one of the great treasures of the Basque Country.

Architectural Allure

The great landmark perched over the Nervión played a pivotal role in transforming the fortunes of this once industrial city. More than two decades after its unveiling, Frank Gehry's shimmering titanium-clad Guggenheim museum has lost none of its ability to captivate. Today though, this artfully designed icon stands among other great architectural works, like the nearby Zubizuri, a soaring bridge designed by Santiago Calatrava, and the Azkuna Zentroa, a wine storage warehouse turned cultural centre that bears the imaginative imprint of Philippe Starck. The city also has its share of beauties from the past, including a neo-baroque theatre, an art nouveau train station and several spectacular cathedrals.

Natural Beauty

Tucked into a lush corner of Northeast Spain, Bilbao is surrounded by rolling green hills, with breathtaking coastline an easy jaunt from town. Parks and plazas dot the city centre, including the Parque de Doña Casilda de Iturrizar with its tree-lined paths and ornamental pond, while riverside promenades give fine views of the cityscape. The heights of Artxanda offer an even more impressive panoramic sweep of the city, and is best reached by the funicular that lumbers its way to the top. Further out, Getxo's beaches and dramatic cliffs make for a spectacular day's outing.

Basque Cuisine

The dining scene in Bilbao staggers the imagination. Here you'll find Michelin-starred eateries, buzzing pintxo bars and long-running family-run restaurants all offering a different take on Basque cuisine. The cobblestone streets of the old town offer endless rewards for foodies, whether munching one's way through the eateries lining the Plaza Nueva or taking in the glimmering food halls of the Mercado de la Ribera. Adding to the bounty is a new crop of appealing cafes and low-lit wine bars, fine spots for unwinding, catching up on local gossip and plotting the next great meal!

Vibrant Culture

Basque culture takes on many forms in this thriving waterfront city. Evocative museums like the Euskal Museoa and the Arkeologi Museo provide a glimpse into centuries past, with their collections of ancient Basque carvings, Middle Age treasures and everyday implements of the mariners, artisans and landowners of this age-old people. Leaping forward a few centuries, the Basque spirit is very much alive in performing arts halls like the Euskalduna Palace or on music-filled stages around town, with Kafe Antzokia serving up the city's latest sounds. Then of course, there's the hallowed Estadio San Mamés, where the 100% Basque team of Athletic Bilbao take the field. The team is a great symbol of Basque pride all across the region.

Experiences in Bilbao

Museo Guggenheim Bilbao

Top choice gallery in New Town

Price - adult/student/child from €16/9/free

Hours - 10am-8pm, closed Mon Sep-Jun

Contact - http://www.guggenheim-bilbao.es; 944 35 90 16

Location - Avenida Abandoibarra 2, Bilbao, Spain

Shimmering titanium Museo Guggenheim Bilbao is one of modern architecture's most iconic buildings. It played a major role in helping to lift Bilbao out of its post-industrial depression and into the 21st century – and with sensation. It sparked the city's inspired regeneration, stimulated further development and placed Bilbao firmly in the international art and tourism spotlight.

Some might say that structure overwhelms function here and that the museum is more famous for its architecture than its content. But Canadian architect Frank Gehry's inspired use of flowing canopies, cliffs, promontories, ship shapes, towers and flying fins is irresistible.

Gehry designed the museum with historical and geographical contexts in mind. The site was an industrial wasteland, part of Bilbao's wretched and decaying warehouse district on the banks of the Ría del Nervión. The city's historical industries of shipbuilding and fishing reflected Gehry's own interests, not least his engagement with industrial materials in previous works. The gleaming titanium tiles that sheathe most of the building like giant herring scales are said to have been inspired by the architect's childhood fascination with fish.

Other artists have added their touch as well. Lying between the glass buttresses of the central atrium and the Ría del Nervión is a simple pool of water that emits a mist installation by Fuyiko Nakaya. Near the riverbank is Louise Bourgeois' Maman, a skeletal spider-like canopy said to symbolise a protective embrace. In the open area west of the museum, the child-favourite fountain sculpture randomly fires off jets of water. Jeff Koons' kitsch whimsy Puppy, a 12m-tall highland terrier made up of thousands of begonias, is on the city side of the museum. Bilbao has hung on to 'El Poop', who was supposed to be a passing attraction as part of a world tour. Bilbaínos will tell you that El Poop came first – and then they had to build a kennel behind it.

Heading inside, the interior is purposefully vast. The cathedral-like atrium is more than 45m high, with light pouring in through the glass cliffs. Permanent exhibitions fill the ground floor and include Richard Serra's massive mazelike sculptures in weathered steel and Jenny Holzer's 9 LED columns of ever-flowing phrases and text fragments (in English, Spanish and Basque) that reach for the skies.

For many people, it is the temporary shows – from retrospectives of the groundbreaking contemporary video artist Bill Viola to wide-ranging exhibitions that explore fin de siècle Paris – that are the main attraction. Excellent self-guided audio tours in various languages are free with admission and there is also a special children's audio guide.

Free guided tours in Spanish take place at 12.30pm and 5pm; sign up half an hour before at the information desk. Tours can be conducted in other languages but you must ask at the information desk beforehand. Groups are limited to 20 (and there needs to be a minimum of eight), so get there early. It's also possible to organise private group tours with in Spanish, English, French and German, among others, by prior arrangement. The museum is equipped with specially adapted magnetic loop PDA video guides for those with hearing impairments.

Entry queues can be horrendous, with wet summer days and Easter almost guaranteeing you a wait of over an hour. The museum is wheelchair accessible.

Casco Viejo

Old town in Old Town

The compact Casco Viejo, Bilbao's atmospheric old quarter, is full of charming streets, boisterous bars and plenty of quirky and independent shops. At the heart of the Casco are Bilbao's original seven streets, Las Siete Calles, which date from the 1400s.

The 14th-century Gothic Catedral de Santiago has a splendid Renaissance portico and pretty little cloister. Further north, the 19th-century arcaded Plaza Nueva is a rewarding pintxo haunt. There's a small Sunday-morning flea market here, which is full of secondhand book and record stalls. In between weave street performers and waiters with trays piled high. The market is much more subdued in winter. A sweeter-smelling flower market takes place on Sunday mornings in the nearby Plaza del Arenal.

Museo de Bellas Artes

Top choice gallery in New Town

Price - adult/student/child €9/7/free, free 10am-3pm Wed & 3-8pm Sun

Hours - 10am-8pm Wed-Mon

Contact - http://www.museobilbao.com; 944 39 60 60

Location - Plaza del Museo 2, Bilbao, Spain

The Museo de Bellas Artes houses a compelling collection that includes everything from Gothic sculptures to 20th-century pop art. There are three main subcollections: classical art, with works by Murillo, Zurbarán, El Greco, Goya and van Dyck; contemporary art, featuring works by Gauguin, Francis Bacon and Anthony Caro; and Basque art, with works of the great sculptors Jorge Oteiza and Eduardo Chillida, and strong paintings by the likes of Ignacio Zuloaga and Juan de Echevarría.

As good as the permanent collection is, it's the temporary exhibitions (see the website for upcoming dates) that really draw the crowds. Past exhibitions have showcased everything from Japanese art to hyperrealist sculpture as well as one of a kind exhibitions, such as Richard Reich's meditative film entitled 'Different Trains'.

Mina Restaurante

Top choice basque in New Town

Price - tasting menu €74-110

Hours - 2-3.30pm Wed-Sun & 9-10.30pm Wed-Sat

Contact - http://www.restaurantemina.es; 944 79 59 38

Location - Muelle Marzana, Bilbao, Spain

Offering unexpected sophistication and fine dining in an otherwise fairly down-at-the-heels neighbourhood, this riverside restaurant has some critics citing it as Bilbao's best. Expect serious culinary creativity: think along the lines of spider crab with passion fruit, aubergine confit with prawns or bone marrow cake with seasonal mushrooms – followed perhaps by saffron crème brûlée.

Reservations are essential.

Euskal Museoa

Museum in Old Town

Price - adult/child €3/free, Thu free

Hours - 10am-7pm Mon & Wed-Fri, 10am-1.30pm & 4-7pm Sat, 10am-2pm Sun

Contact - http://www.euskal-museoa.eus; 944 15 54 23

Location - Plaza Miguel Unamuno 4, Bilbao, Spain

One of Spain's best museums devoted to Basque culture takes visitors on a journey from Paleolithic days to the 21st century, giving an overview of life among the boat builders, mariners, shepherds and artists who have left their mark on modern Basque identity. Displays of clothing, looms, fishing nets, model boats, woodcutter's axes, sheep bells and navigational instruments illustrate everyday life, while iconic round funerary stones help segue into topics of Basque rituals and beliefs.

Don't miss the photographs of Eulalia Abaitua Allende-Salazar, whose black-and-white images of fishmongers, pastoral families and dock workers capture early 20th-century Basque life. The museum is housed in a fine old building that was part of an original 17th-century Jesuit college. In the cloister is the Mikeldi Idol, a powerful pre-Christian symbolic figure, possibly from the Iron Age. Found near Durango, this zoomorphic sculpture was carved from a single block of sandstone and retains an element of pure mystery.

Signage is in Spanish and Euskara, though rooms have handouts with English translations of some of the sections.

Museo Marítimo Ría de Bilbao

Museum in New Town

Price - adult/child €6/3.50, free Tue Sep-Jun

Hours - 10am-8pm Tue-Sun, to 6pm Oct-Mar

Contact - http://www.museomaritimobilbao.org

Location - Muelle Ramón de la Sota 1, Bilbao, Spain

This interactive maritime museum, appropriately situated down on the waterfront, uses bright and well-designed displays to bring the watery depths of Bilbao and Basque maritime history to life. Start off by watching the 10-minute video which gives an overview of Bilbao history from the 1300s to the present, then wander through the two floors of displays, which show old shipbuilidng techniques, harrowing shipwrecks (and innovative coastal rescue strategies), pirate threats and artfully designed models – including a full-scale recreation of the 1511 Consulate Barge.

Don't miss the 'Sculpture of Light', an audiovisual installation that shows the profound changes Bilbao underwent from the mid 1980s to 2010. There's also an outdoor section where children (and nautically inclined grown-ups) can clamber about a range of boats pretending to be pirates and sailors. It's worth downloading the free iPhone app (Museo Marítimo Ría de Bilbao), which provides insightful commentary on many exhibits in the museum.

Azkuna Zentroa (Alhóndiga)

Architecture in New Town

Hours - 7am-11pm Mon-Fri, from 8.30am Sat & Sun

Contact - http://www.azkunazentroa.com, 944 01 40 14

Location - Plaza Alhóndiga 4, Bilbao, Spain

Take a neglected wine storage warehouse, convert it into a leisure and cultural centre, add a bit of Bilbao style and the result is the Azkuna Zentroa (Alhóndiga). Designed by renowned architect Philippe Starck, it now houses a cinema, an art gallery, a rooftop swimming pool with a glass bottom, a public media centre, cafes and restaurants. The ground floor is notable for its 43 tubby columns, each constructed with a unique design.

Arkeologi Museo

Museum in Old Town

Price - adult/student/child €3/1.50/free, Fri free

Hours - 10am-2pm & 4-7.30pm Tue-Sat

Location - Calzadas de Mallona 2, Bilbao, Spain

This two-story museum takes you deep into the past, beginning with fossils found in the Sierra de Atapuerca a mere 430,000(!) years ago. Along the romp through the ages, you'll see models of early fortified villages, Celt-Iberian carvings, and statues and fragments from the Roman period before descending (start on the second floor) into the Visigothic times and the ensuing Middle Ages. Stones for catapaults, a 10th-century trephined skull and jewellery from the 1200s are other curiosities.

The signature piece is a 12m-long sailboat – substantial fragments of the vessel at least – dating from the 15th century, which shows just how long the Basque people have had this obsession with the sea.

Interactive touch screens give details (in Spanish or Basque) on tool creation, funerary rites and rock carvings. Unfortunately, labelling is in Spanish and Basque only, though there is an audioguide for Android users.

Basilica de Begoña

Basilica in Bilbao

Hours - 9am-1.30pm & 5-8.30pm Mon-Sat, 9am-2pm & 5-9pm Sun

Location - Calle Virgen de Begoña, Bilbao, Spain

This 16th-century basilica towers over the Casco Viejo from atop a nearby hill. It's mainly Gothic in look, although Renaissance touches, such as the arched main entrance, crept in during its century-long construction. The austere vaulted interior is brightened by a gold altarpiece which contains a statue of the Virgin Begoña, the patron saint of Biscay who's venerated locally as Amatxu (Mother).

To get to the basilica either take the elevator from the Casco Viejo metro station or climb the stairs from Plaza Unamuno.

Alicante

Of all Spain's mainland provincial capitals, Alicante is the most influenced by tourism, thanks to the nearby airport and resorts. Nevertheless this is a dynamic, attractive Spanish city with a castle, old quarter and long waterfront. The eating scene is exciting and the nightlife is absolutely legendary, whether you're chugging pints with the stag parties at 7pm or twirling on the dance floor with the locals seven hours later. On a weekend night it's impossibly busy and buzzy year-round.

Experiences in Alicante

Museo Arqueológico Provincial

Top choice museum in Alicante

Price - adult/child €3/1.50

Hours - 10am-7pm Tue-Fri, 10am-8.30pm Sat, 10am-2pm Sun Sep-Jun, 10am-2pm & 6-10pm Tue-Sat, 10am-2pm Sun Jul-Oct

Contact - http://www.marqalicante.com; 965 14 90 00

Location - Plaza Dr Gómez Ulla, Alicante, Spain

This museum has a strong collection of ceramics and Iberian art. Exhibits are displayed to give the visitor a very visual, high-tech experience, and it's all beautifully presented. The only drawback is the lack of information in English.

Museo de Arte Contemporáneo de Alicante

Top choice gallery in Alicante

Hours - 10am-8pm Tue-Sat, to 2pm Sun

Contact - http://www.maca-alicante.es

Location - Plaza Santa María 3; Alicante, Spain

This splendid museum, inside the 17th-century Casa de la Asegurada, has an excellent collection of 20th-century Spanish art, including works by Dalí, Miró, Chillida, Sempere, Tàpies and Picasso.

Playa de San Juan

Beach in Alicante

Northeast of the town, Playa de San Juan, easily reached by the tram (Costa Blanca stop), is larger and usually less crowded than the city beach.

Castillo de Santa Bárbara

Castle in Alicante

Hours - 10am-10pm Apr-Sep, to 8pm Oct-Mar

Contact - http://www.castillodesantabarbara.com; 965 92 77 15

Location - Calle Vázquez de Mella, Alicante, Spain

There are sweeping views over the city from this large 16th-century castle, which houses a museum recounting the history of the city and containing a couple of chambers with temporary exhibitions. It's a sweaty walk up the hill to the castle, but there's a lift that rises through the bowels of the mountain to the summit. To return, it's a pleasant stroll down through Parque de la Ereta.

Lucentum

Archaeological site in Alicante

Price - adult/child €2/free

Hours - 9am-noon & 6-9pm Tue-Sat, 9am-noon Sun mid-Jun–mid-Sep, 10am-2pm & 4-6pm Tue-Sat, 10am-2pm Sun mid-Sep–mid-Jun

Contact - http://www.marqalicante.com; 965 14 90 00

Location - Calle Zeus, Alicante, Spain

The Roman town of Lucentum, a forerunner of Alicante, is where excavations have revealed a rich wealth of pottery. You can make out its clearly defined streets and town plan, as well as bathhouses, the forum, a large house with columned courtyard and various other dwellings.

Museu de Fogueres

Museum in Alicante

Hours - 10am-2pm & 5-8pm or 6-9pm Tue-Sat, 10am-2pm Sun

Contact - 965 14 68 28

Location - Rambla de Méndez Núñez 29, Alicante, Spain

In addition to a wealth of photographs, costumes and ninots (small effigies saved from the flames), this museum has a great audiovisual presentation of what the Fiesta de Sant Joan, all fire and partying, means to alicantinos.

Córdoba

One building alone is reason enough to put Córdoba high on your itinerary: the mesmerising multiarched Mezquita. One of the world's greatest Islamic buildings, the Mezquita is a symbol of the worldly, sophisticated culture that flourished here more than a millennium ago when Córdoba was capital of Islamic Spain and western Europe's biggest, most cultured city. But today's Córdoba is much more than the Mezquita. With a lot to see and do, some charming accommodation, and excellent restaurants and bars, it merits far more than the fleeting visit many travellers give it. Córdoba's real charms unfold as you explore the winding, stone-paved lanes of the medieval city to the west, north and east of the gaudy touristic area immediately around the Mezquita, wandering between wrought-iron balconies and lamps, potted plants, overhanging trees, golden-stone buildings and verdant interior patios, emerging every few minutes on yet another quaint little hidden plaza.

Experinces in Córdoba

Mezquita

Top choice mosque in Córdoba

Price - adult/child €10/5, 8.30-9.30am Mon-Sat free

Hours - 8.30-9.30am & 10am-7pm Mon-Sat & 8.30-11.30am & 3-7pm Sun Mar-Oct, 8.30-9.30am & 10am-6pm Mon-Sat & 8.30-11.30am & 3-6pm Sun Nov-Feb

Contact - http://www.mezquita-catedraldecordoba.es; 957 47 05 12

Location - Calle Cardenal Herrero, Córdoba, Spain

It's impossible to overemphasise the beauty of Córdoba's great mosque, with its remarkably serene (despite tourist crowds) and spacious interior.

One of the world's greatest works of Islamic architecture, the Mezquita hints, with all its lustrous decoration, at a refined age when Muslims, Jews and Christians lived side by side and enriched their city with a heady interaction of diverse, vibrant cultures.

Arab chronicles recount how Abd ar-Rahman I purchased half of the Visigothic church of San Vicente for the Muslim community's Friday prayers, and then, in AD 784, bought the other half on which to erect a new mosque. Three later extensions nearly quintupled the size of Abd ar-Rahman I's mosque and brought it to the form you see today – with one major alteration: a Christian cathedral plonked right in the middle of the mosque in the 16th century (hence the often-used description 'Mezquita-Catedral').

Mass is celebrated in the central cathedral at 9.30am Monday to Saturday, and at noon and 1.30pm Sundays.

Patio de los Naranjos

This lovely courtyard, with its orange, palm and cypress trees and fountains, forms the entrance to the Mezquita. It was the site of ritual ablutions before prayer in the mosque. Its most impressive entrance is the Puerta del Perdón, a 14th-century Mudéjar archway next to the bell tower. The Mezquita's ticket office is just inside here.

Belltower (Torre Campanari)

You can climb the 54m-high belltower for fine panoramas and an interesting bird's-eye angle on the main Mezquita building. Up to 20 people are allowed up the tower every half-hour from 9.30am to 1.30pm and 4pm to 6.30pm (to 5.30pm November to February; no afternoon visits in July or August). Tickets (€2) are sold on the inner side of the Puerta del Perdón, next to the tower: they often sell out well ahead of visit times, so it's a good idea to buy them early in the day. Originally built by Abd ar-Rahman III in 951–52 as the Mezquita's minaret, the tower was encased in a strengthened outer shell, and heightened, by the

Christians in the 16th and 17th centuries. You can still see some caliphal vaults and arches inside.

The original minaret would have looked something like the Giralda in Seville, which was practically a copy. Córdoba's minaret influenced all minarets built thereafter throughout the western Islamic world.

The Mezquita's Interior

The Mezquita's architectural uniqueness and importance lies in the fact that, structurally speaking, it was a revolutionary building for its time. Earlier major Islamic buildings such as the Dome of the Rock in Jerusalem and the Great Mosque in Damascus placed an emphasis on verticality, but the Mezquita was intended as a democratically horizontal and simple space, where the spirit could be free to roam and communicate easily with God – a kind of glorious refinement of the original simple Islamic prayer space (usually the open yard of a desert home).

Men prayed side by side on the argamasa, a floor made of compact, reddish slaked lime and sand. A flat roof, decorated with gold and multicoloured motifs, was supported by striped arches suggestive of a forest of date palms. The arches rested on, eventually, 1293 columns (of which 856 remain today). Useful leaflets in several languages are available free just inside the door by which visitors enter.

Abd ar-Rahman I's initial prayer hall – the area immediately inside today's visitor entrance – was divided into 11 'naves' by lines of arches striped in red brick and white stone. The columns of these arches were a mishmash of material collected from the earlier church on the site, Córdoba's Roman buildings and places as far away as Constantinople. To raise the ceiling high enough to create a sense of openness, inventive builders came up with the idea of a two-tier construction, using taller columns as a base and planting shorter ones on top.

Later enlargements of the mosque, southward by Abd ar-Rahman II in the 9th century and Al-Hakim II in the 960s, and eastward by Al-Mansur in the 970s, extended it to an area of nearly 14,400 sq metres, making it one of the biggest mosques in the world. The arcades' simplicity and number give a sense of endlessness to the Mezquita.

The final Mezquita had 19 doors along its north side, filling it with light and yielding a sense of openness. Nowadays, nearly all these doorways are closed off, dampening the vibrant effect of the red-and-white double arches. Christian additions to the building, such as the solid mass of the cathedral in the centre and the 50 or so chapels around the fringes, further enclose and impose on the airy space.

Mihrab & Maksura

Like Abd ar-Rahman II a century earlier, Al-Hakim II in the 960s lengthened the naves of the prayer hall, creating a new qiblah wall (indicating the direction of Mecca) and mihrab (prayer niche) at the south end. The bay immediately in front of the mihrab and the bays to each side form the maksura, the area where the caliphs and courtiers would have prayed. The mihrab and maksura are the most beautifully and intricately decorated parts of the whole mosque.

The greatest glory of Al-Hakim II's extension was the portal of the mihrab – a crescent arch with a rectangular surround known as an alfiz. For the portal's decoration, Al-Hakim asked the emperor of Byzantium, Nicephoras II Phocas, to send him a mosaicist capable of imitating the superb mosaics of the Great Mosque of Damascus, one of the great 8th-century Syrian Umayyad buildings. The Christian emperor sent the Muslim caliph not only a mosaicist but also a gift of 1600kg of gold mosaic cubes. Shaped into flower motifs and inscriptions from the Quran, this gold is what gives the mihrab portal its magical glitter. Inside the mihrab, a single block of white marble sculpted into the shape of a scallop shell, a symbol of the Quran, forms the dome that amplified the voice of the imam (the person who leads Islamic worship services) throughout the mosque.

The arches of the maksura are the mosque's most intricate and sophisticated, forming a forest of interwoven horseshoe shapes. Equally attractive are the maksura's skylit domes, decorated with star-patterned stone vaulting. Each dome is held up by four interlocking pairs of parallel ribs, a highly advanced technique for 10th-century Europe.

Cathedral

Following the Christian conquest of Córdoba in 1236, the Mezquita was used as a cathedral but remained largely unaltered for nearly three centuries. But in the 16th century King Carlos I gave the cathedral authorities permission to rip out the centre of the Mezquita in order to construct a new Capilla Mayor (main altar area) and coro (choir).

Legend has it that when the king saw the result he was horrified, exclaiming that the builders had destroyed something unique in the world. The cathedral took nearly 250 years to complete (1523–1766) and thus exhibits a range of architectural fashions, from plateresque and late Renaissance to extravagant Spanish baroque. Among the later features are the Capilla Mayor's rich 17th-century jasper and red-marble retable (altar screen), and the fine mahogany stalls in the choir, carved in the 18th century by Pedro Duque Cornejo.

Night Visits

A one-hour sound-and-light show (www.elalmadecordoba.com), in nine languages via audioguides, is presented in the Mezquita twice nightly except Sundays from March to October, and on Friday and Saturday from November to February. Tickets are €18 (senior or student €9).

Palacio de Viana

Top choice museum in Córdoba

Price - whole house/patios €8/5

Hours - 10am-7pm Tue-Sat & to 3pm Sun Sep-Jun, 9am-3pm Tue-Sun Jul & Aug

Contact - http://www.palaciodeviana.com

Location - Plaza de Don Gome 2, Córdoba, Spain

A stunning Renaissance palace with 12 beautiful, plant-filled patios, the Viana Palace is a particular delight to visit in spring. Occupied by the aristocratic Marqueses de Viana until 1980, the large building is packed with art and antiques. You can just walk round the lovely patios and garden with a self-guiding leaflet, or take a guided tour of the rooms as well. It's an 800m walk northeast from Plaza de las Tendillas.

Medina Azahara

Archaeological site in Córdoba

Price - EU citizen/other free/€1.50

Hours - 9am-7pm Tue-Sat Apr–mid-Jun, to 3pm mid-Jun–mid-Sep, to 6pm mid-Sep–Mar, 9am-3pm Sun year-round

Contact - http://www.museosdeandalucia.es; 957 10 49 33

Location - Carretera Palma del Río Km 5.5, Córdoba, Spain

Eight kilometres west of Córdoba stands what's left of Medina Azahara, the sumptuous palace-city built by Caliph Abd ar-Rahman III in the 10th century. The complex spills down a hillside, with the caliph's palace (the area you visit today) on the highest levels overlooking what were gardens and open fields. The residential areas (still unexcavated) were set away to each side. A fascinating modern museum has been installed below the site.

Legend has it that Abd ar-Rahman III built Medina Azahara for his favourite wife, Az-Zahra. Dismayed by her homesickness and yearnings for the snowy mountains of Syria, he surrounded his new city with almond and cherry trees, replacing snowflakes with fluffy white blossoms. More realistically, it was probably Abd ar-Rahman's declaration of his caliphate in 929 that spurred him to construct, as caliphs were wont to do, a new capital. Building started in 940 and chroniclers record some staggering statistics: 10,000 labourers set 6000 stone blocks a day, with outer walls stretching 1518m east to west and 745m north to south.

It is almost inconceivable to think that such a city, built over 35 years, was to last only a few more before the usurper Al-Mansur transferred government to a new palace complex of his own in 981. Then, between 1010 and 1013, Madinat al-Zahra was wrecked by Berber soldiers. During succeeding centuries its ruins were plundered repeatedly for building materials.

From the museum, where you arrive and get tickets for the site (and where you must park if coming in your own vehicle), a shuttle bus (lanzadera; adult/child/senior €2.10/1.50/1.50 return) takes you 2km up to the top of the site. The visitors' route then leads down through the city's original northern gate. Highlights of the visitable area are the grand, arched Edificio Basilical Superior, which housed the main state admin offices, and the Casa de Yafar, believed to have been residence of the caliph's prime minister. The crown jewel of the site, the royal reception hall known as the Salón de Abd ar-Rahman III (or Salón Rico), has been closed for restoration since 2009 (with no expected completion date at the time of research). This hall has exquisitely carved stucco work and is said to have been decorated with gold and silver tiles, arches of ivory and ebony, and walls of multicoloured marble.

The museum takes you through the history of Medina Azahara, with sections on its planning and construction, its inhabitants and its eventual downfall – all illustrated with beautifully displayed pieces from the site and interactive displays, and complemented by flawless English translations.

Drivers should leave Córdoba westward along Avenida de Medina Azahara. This feeds into the A431 road, with the turn-off to Madinat al-Zahra signposted after 6km.

A bus to Medina Azahara (adult/child €9/5 return including the shuttle from museum to site and back) leaves from a stop on Glorieta Cruz Roja near Córdoba's Puerta de Almodóvar at 10.15am and 11am Tuesday to Sunday, plus 2.45pm Tuesday to Saturday from mid-September to mid-June. You can get tickets on the bus, or in advance at tourist offices. Buying in advance is sensible for weekends and public holidays. The bus starts back back from Medina Azahara hours after it leaves Córdoba.

An interesting alternative way of getting here is on an electric-bicycle tour with Elektrik.es. English- or Spanish-language guided visits with Córdoba Visión are offered for €20 (children €10), using the 10.15am bus service; get tickets in advance through its office or tourist offices.

Centro Flamenco Fosforito

Top choice museum in Córdoba

Hours - 8.30am-3pm Tue-Sun mid-Jun–mid-Sep, 8.30am-7.30pm Tue-Fr & 8.30am-2.30pm Sat & Sun mid-Sep–mid-Jun

Contact - http://www.centroflamencofosforito.cordoba.es; 957 47 68 29

Location - Plaza del Potro, Córdoba, Spain

Possibly the best flamenco museum in Andalucía, the Fosforito centre has exhibits, film and information panels in English and Spanish telling you the history of the guitar and all the flamenco greats. Touch-screen videos demonstrate the important techniques of flamenco song, guitar, dance and percussion – you can test your skill at beating out the compás (rhythm) of different palos (song forms). Regular free live flamenco performances are held here, too, often at noon on Sundays (listed on the website).

The museum benefits from a fantastic location inside the Posada del Potro, a legendary inn that played a part in Don Quijote, where Cervantes described it as a 'den of thieves'. The famous square it stands on, once a horse market, features a lovely 16th-century stone fountain topped by a rearing potro (colt).

Alcázar de los Reyes Cristianos

Fortress in Córdoba

Price - adult/student/child €4.50/2.25/free

Hours - 8.30am-3pm Tue-Sat & to 2.30pm Sun mid-Jun–mid-Sep, 8.30am-8.45pm Tue-Fri, to 4.30pm Sat & to 2.30pm Sun mid-Sep–mid-Jun

Contact - http://www.alcazardelosreyescristianos.cordoba.es; 957 42 01 51

Location - Campo Santo de Los Mártires, Córdoba, Spain

Built under Castilian rule in the 13th and 14th centuries on the remains of a Moorish predecessor, this fort-cum-palace was where the Catholic Monarchs, Fernando and Isabel, made their first acquaintance with Columbus in 1486. One hall displays some remarkable Roman mosaics, dug up from Plaza de la Corredera in the 1950s. The Alcázar's terraced gardens – full of fish ponds, fountains, orange trees and flowers – are a delight to stroll around.

At 9pm (except Mondays) there's a popular multimedia show featuring lights, flamenco music and dancing fountains called Noches Mágicas en el Alcázar (Magic Nights in the Alcázar; adult/child €6.50/free). While here, it's also interesting to visit the nearby Baños del Alcázar Califal, the impressive 10th-century bathhouse of the Moorish Alcázar.

Granada

Drawn by the allure of the Alhambra, many visitors head to Granada unsure what to expect. What they find is a gritty, compelling city where serene Islamic architecture and Arab-flavoured street life go hand in hand with monumental churches, old-school tapas bars and counterculture graffiti art.

The city, sprawled at the foot of the Sierra Nevada, was the last stronghold of the Spanish Moors and their legacy lies all around: it's in the horseshoe arches, the spicy aromas emanating from street stalls, the teterías (teahouses) of the Albayzín, the historic Arab quarter. Most spectacularly, of course, it's in the Alhambra, an astonishing palace complex whose Islamic decor and landscaped gardens are without peer in Europe.

There's also an energy to Granada's streets, packed as they are with bars, student dives, bohemian cafes and intimate flamenco clubs, and it's this as much as the more traditional sights that leaves a lasting impression.

Experiences in Granada

Alhambra

Top choice islamic palace in Granada

Price - adult/12-15yr/under 12yr €14/8/free, Generalife & Alcazaba adult/under 12yr €7/free

Hours - 8.30am-8pm Apr–mid-Oct, to 6pm mid-Oct–Mar, night visits 10-11.30pm Tue-Sat Apr–mid-Oct, 8-9.30pm Fri & Sat mid-Oct–Mar

Contact - http://alhambra-patronato.es; 858 95 36 16; 958 02 79 71

Location - Granada, Spain

The Alhambra is Granada's – and Europe's – love letter to Moorish culture. Set against a backdrop of brooding Sierra Nevada peaks, this fortified palace complex started life as a walled citadel before going on to become the opulent seat of Granada's Nasrid emirs. Their showpiece palaces, the 14th-century Palacios Nazaríes, are among the finest Islamic buildings in Europe and, together with the gorgeous Generalife gardens, form the Alhambra's great headline act.

As one of Spain's most high-profile attractions, the Alhambra can draw up to 6000 daily visitors. Tickets sell out quickly so to avoid disappointment it pays to book ahead, either online or by phone. Note that when you buy a ticket you'll be given a time to enter the Palacio Nazaríes, admission to which is strictly controlled. For more information, see Alhambra Practicalities.

The origins of the Alhambra, whose name derives from the Arabic al-qala'a al-hamra (the Red Castle), are mired in mystery. The first references to construction in the area appear in the 9th century but it's thought that buildings may already have been standing since Roman times. In its current form, it largely dates to the 13th and 14th centuries when Granada's Nasrid rulers transformed it into a fortified palace complex. Following the 1492 Reconquista (Christian reconquest), its mosque was replaced by a church and the Habsburg emperor Charles V had a wing of palaces demolished to make space for the huge Renaissance building that still today bears his name. Later, in the early 19th century, French Napoleonic forces destroyed part of the palace and attempted to blow up the entire site. Restoration work began in the mid-1800s and continues to this day.

Palacio de Carlos V

From the entrance pavilion, a signposted path leads into the core of the complex, passing a couple of notable religious buildings. The first is the Convento de San Francisco, now the Parador de Granada hotel, where the bodies of Isabel and Fernando were laid to rest while their tombs were being built in the Capilla Real. A short walk further on brings you to the Iglesia de Santa María de la Alhambra, a 16th-century church on the site of the Alhambra's original mosque.

Beyond the church, the Palacio de Carlos V clashes spectacularly with the style of its surroundings. The hulking palace, begun in 1527 by the Toledo architect Pedro Machuca, features a monumental facade and a two-tiered circular courtyard ringed by 32 columns. This circle inside a square is the only Spanish example of a Renaissance ground plan symbolising the unity of heaven and earth.

Inside the palace are two museums: the Museo de la Alhambra, which showcases an absorbing collection of Islamic artefacts, including the door from the Sala de Dos Hermanas; and the Museo de Bellas Artes, home to a collection of 15th- to 20th-century artworks.

Alcazaba

Occupying the western tip of the Alhambra are the martial remnants of the Alcazaba, the site's original 13th-century citadel. The Torre de la Vela (Watchtower) is famous as the tower where the cross and banners of the Reconquista were raised in January 1492. A winding staircase leads to the top where you can enjoy sweeping views over Granada's rooftops.

Palacios Nazaríes

The Alhambra's stunning centrepiece, the palace complex known as the Palacios Nazaríes, was originally divided into three sections: the Mexuar, a chamber for administrative and public business; the Palacio de Comares, the emir's official and private residence; and the Palacio de los Leones, a private area for the royal family and harem.

Entrance is through the Mexuar, a 14th-century hall where the council of ministers would sit and the emir would adjudicate citizens' appeals. Two centuries later, it was converted into a chapel, with a prayer room at the far end. Look up here and elsewhere to appreciate the geometrically carved wood ceilings.

From the Mexuar, you pass into the Patio del Cuarto Dorado, a courtyard where the emirs gave audiences, with the Cuarto Dorado (Golden Room) on the left. Opposite the Cuarto Dorado is the entrance to the Palacio de Comares through a beautiful facade of glazed tiles, stucco and carved wood. A dogleg corridor (a common strategy in Islamic architecture to keep interior rooms private) leads through to the Patio de los Arrayanes (Court of the Myrtles). This elegant patio, named after the myrtle hedges around its rectangular pool, is the central space of the palace that was built in the mid-14th century as Emir Yusuf I's official residence.

The southern end of the patio is overshadowed by the walls of the Palacio de Carlos V. To the north, in the 45m-high Torre de Comares (Comares Tower), the Sala de la Barca (Hall of the Blessing) leads into the Salón de los Embajadores (Chamber of the Ambassadors), where the emirs would have conducted negotiations with Christian emissaries. The room's marvellous domed marquetry ceiling contains more than 8000 cedar pieces in an intricate star pattern representing the seven heavens of Islam.

The Patio de los Arrayanes leads into the Palacio de los Leones (Palace of the Lions), built in the second half of the 14th century under Muhammad V. The palace rooms branch off the Patio de los Leones (Lion Courtyard), centred on an 11th-century fountain channelling water through the mouths of 12 marble lions. The courtyard layout, using the proportions of the golden ratio, demonstrates the complexity of Islamic geometric design – the 124 slender columns that support the ornamented pavilions are placed in such a way that they are symmetrical on numerous axes.

Of the four halls around the patio, the southern Sala de los Abencerrajes is the most impressive. Boasting a mesmerising octagonal stalactite ceiling, this is the legendary site of the murders of the noble Abencerraj family, whose leader, the story goes, dared to dally with Zoraya, Abu al-Hasan's favourite concubine. The rusty stains in the fountain are said to be the victims' indelible blood.

At the eastern end of the patio is the Sala de los Reyes (Hall of the Kings) with a leather-lined ceiling painted by 14th-century Christian artists. The hall's name comes from the painting on the central alcove, thought to depict 10 Nasrid emirs.

On the patio's northern side is the richly decorated Sala de Dos Hermanas (Hall of Two Sisters), probably named after the slabs of white marble flanking its fountain. It features a dizzying muqarnas (honeycomb vaulted) dome with a central star and 5000 tiny cells, reminiscent of the constellations. This may have been the room of the emir's favourite paramour. The carved wood screens in the upper level enabled women (and perhaps others involved in palace intrigue) to peer down from hallways above without being seen. At its far end, the tile-trimmed Mirador de Daraxa (Daraxa lookout) was a lovely place for palace denizens to look onto the garden below.

From the Sala de Dos Hermanas, a passageway leads through the Estancias del Emperador (Emperor's Chambers), built for Carlos I in the

1520s, and later used by the American author Washington Irving. From here descend to the Patio de la Reya (Patio of the Grille) and the Patio de la Lindaraja, where, in the southwest corner you can peer into the bathhouse lit by star-shaped skylights.

You eventually emerge into the Jardines del Partal, an area of terraced gardens laid out at the beginning of the 20th century. Here a reflecting pool stands in front of the Palacio del Partal, a small porticoed building with its own tower (the Torre de las Dameas) dating to the early 14th century. Leave the Partal gardens by a gate facing the Palacio de Carlos V, or continue along a path to the Generalife.

Generalife

The Generalife, the sultans' gorgeous summer estate, dates to the 14th century. A soothing ensemble of pathways, patios, pools, fountains, trees and, in season, flowers of every imaginable hue, it takes its name from the Arabic jinan al-'arif, meaning 'the overseer's gardens'.

A string of elegant rectangular plots, the Jardines Nuevos, leads up to the whitewashed Palacio del Generalife, the emirs' summer palace. The courtyards here are particularly graceful – in the second one, the Patio delCiprés de la Sultana, the trunk of a 700-year-old cypress tree suggests what delicate shade would once have graced the area. Beyond the courtyard, a staircase known as the Escalera del Agua is a delightful work of landscape engineering with water channels running down the shaded steps.

Mirador San Nicolás

Top choice viewpoint in Granada

Location - Plaza de San Nicolás, Granada, Spain

This is the place for those classic sunset shots of the Alhambra sprawled along a wooded hilltop with the dark Sierra Nevada mountains looming in the background. It's a well-known spot, accessible via Callejón de San Cecilio, so expect crowds of camera-toting tourists, students and buskers. It's also a haunt of pickpockets and bag-snatchers, so keep your wits about you as you enjoy the views.

Basílica San Juan de Díos

Top choice basilica in Granada

Price - admission €4

Hours - 10am-1.30pm Mon-Sat & 4-6.45pm Sun

Contact - http://www.sjdgranada.es

Location - Calle San Juan de Díos 19, Granada, Spain

Head to this historic basilica, built between 1737 and 1759, for a blinding display of opulent baroque decor. Barely a square inch of its interior lacks embellishment, most of it in gleaming gold and silver. Frescoes by Diego Sánchez Sarabia and the Neapolitan painter Conrado Giaquinto adorn the ceilings and side-chapels, whilst up above the basilica's dome soars to a height of 50m. The highlight, however, is the extraordinary gold altarpiece in the Capilla Mayor.

Once you've taken in the head-spinning details, search out a staff member to accompany you up the stairs behind the altar to where St John of God's remains are set deep in a niche surrounded by gold, gold and yet more gold.

Capilla Real

Top choice historic building in Granada

Price - adult/student/child €5/3.50/free

Hours - 10.15am-6.30pm Mon-Sat, 11am-6.30pm Sun

Contact - http://www.capillarealgranada.com; 958 22 78 48

Location - Calle Oficios, Granada, Spain

The Royal Chapel is the last resting place of Spain's Reyes Católicos (Catholic Monarchs), Isabella I of Castile (1451–1504) and Ferdinand II of Aragon (1452–1516). The royal couple commissioned the elaborate Isabelline-Gothic-style mausoleum that was to house them, but it wasn't completed until 1517, hence their interment in the Alhambra's Convento de San Francisco until 1521.

Their monumental marble tombs, together with those of their heirs, lie in the chancel, behind a gilded wrought-iron screen, created by Bartolomé de Jaén in 1520.

However, the tombs are just for show as the monarchs actually lie in simple lead coffins in the crypt beneath the chancel. Also there are the coffins of Isabel and Fernando's unfortunate daughter, Juana the Mad, her husband, Philip of Flanders, and Miguel, Prince of Asturias, who died as a boy.

The sacristy contains a small but impressive museum, with Fernando's sword and Isabel's sceptre, silver crown and personal art collection, which is mainly Flemish but also includes Botticelli's Prayer in the Garden of Olives. Felipe de Vigarni's two early-16th-century statues of the Catholic Monarchs at prayer are also here.

Palacios Nazaríes

Islamic palace in Granada

Price - adult/12-15yr/under 12yr €14/8/free

Hours - 8.30am-8pm Apr–mid-Oct, to 6pm mid-Oct–Mar, night visits 10-11.30pm Tue-Sat Apr–mid-Oct, 8-9.30pm Fri & Sat mid-Oct–Mar

Contact - http://alhambra-patronato.es; 958 02 79 71

Location - Calle de Real de Alhama, Granada, Spain

This is the stunning centrepiece of the Alhambra, the most brilliant Islamic building in Europe, with perfectly proportioned rooms and courtyards, intricately moulded stucco walls, beautiful tiling, fine carved wooden ceilings and elaborate stalactite-like muqarnas vaulting, all worked in mesmerising, symbolic, geometrical patterns. Arabic inscriptions proliferate in the stucco work.

Admission to the palacios is strictly controlled and when you buy your Alhambra ticket you'll be given a time to enter. Once inside, you can stay as long as you like.

The palace was originally divided into three main areas: the Mexuar, the administrative and public part of the complex; the Palacio Comares, the emir's official residence; and the Palacio de los Leones, his private quarters.

Entrance is through the Mexuar, a 14th-century room used as a ministerial council chamber and antechamber for those awaiting audiences with the emir. The public would have gone no further.

From the Mexuar you pass into the Patio del Cuarto Dorado, a courtyard where the emirs gave audiences, with the Cuarto Dorado (Golden Room) on the left. Opposite the Cuarto Dorado is the entrance to the Palacio de Comares through a beautiful facade of glazed tiles, stucco and carved wood.

Built for Emir Yusuf I, the Palacio de Comares served as his official residence. It's set around the lovely Patio de los Arrayanes (Patio of the Myrtles) with its rectangular pool. The southern end of the patio is overshadowed by the walls of the Palacio de Carlos V. Inside the northern Torre de Comares (Comares Tower), the Sala de la Barca (Hall of the Blessing) leads into the Salón de los Embajadores (Chamber of the Ambassadors), where the emirs would have conducted negotiations with Christian emissaries. This room's marvellous domed marquetry ceiling contains more than 8000 cedar pieces in a pattern of stars representing the seven heavens of Islam.

The Patio de los Arrayanes leads into the Palacio de los Leones (Palace of the Lions), built in the second half of the 14th century under

Muhammad V. The palace rooms surround the famous Patio de los Leones (Lion Courtyard), with its marble fountain channelling water through the mouths of 12 marble lions. The courtyard layout, using the proportions of the golden ratio, demonstrates the complexity of Islamic geometric design – the 124 slender columns that support the ornamented pavilions are placed in such a way that they are symmetrical on numerous axes.

Of the four halls around the patio, the southern Sala de los Abencerrajes is the most spectacular. Boasting a mesmerising octagonal stalactite ceiling, this is the legendary site of the murders of the noble Abencerraj family, whose leader, the story goes, dared to dally with Zoraya, Abu al-Hasan's favourite concubine. The rusty stains in the fountain are said to be the victims' indelible blood. At the eastern end of the patio is the Sala de los Reyes (Hall of the Kings) with a leather-lined ceiling painted by 14th-century Christian artists. The name comes from the painting on the central alcove, thought to depict 10 Nasrid emirs. On the northern side of the patio is the richly decorated Sala de Dos Hermanas (Hall of Two Sisters), probably named after the slabs of white marble flanking its fountain. It features a fantastic muqarnas dome with a central star and 5000 tiny cells, reminiscent of the constellations. This may have been the room of the emir's favourite paramour. At its far end, the tile-trimmed Mirador de Daraxa (Daraxa lookout) was a lovely place for palace denizens to look onto the garden below.

From the Sala de Dos Hermanas a passage leads through the Estancias del Emperador (Emperor's Chambers), built for Carlos I in the 1520s, and later used by the American author Washington Irving. From here, descend to the Patio de la Reja (Patio of the Grille) and Patio de Lindaraja before emerging into the Jardines del Partal, an area of terraced gardens. Leave the Partal gardens by a gate facing the Palacio de Carlos V, or continue along a path to the Generalife.

The Palacios Nazaríes are also open for night visits.

Sala de Dos Hermanas

Architecture in Granada

Price - adult/12-15yr/under 12yr €14/8/free

Hours - 8.30am-8pm Apr–mid-Oct, to 6pm mid-Oct–Mar, night visits 10-11.30pm Tue-Sat Apr–mid-Oct, 8-9.30pm Fri & Sat mid-Oct–Mar

Contact - http://alhambra-patronato.es; 958 02 79 71

Location - Granada, Spain

The richly decorated Sala de Dos Hermanas (Hall of Two Sisters), in the Palacios Nazaríes section of the Alhambra, sits on the northern side of the Patio de los Leones. Probably named after the slabs of white marble flanking its fountain, it features a dizzying muqarnas (honeycomb vaulted) dome with a central star and 5000 tiny cells, reminiscent of the constellations. This may have been the room of the emir's favourite paramour.

The carved wood screens in the upper level enabled women (and perhaps others involved in palace intrigue) to peer down from hallways above without being seen. At its far end, the tile-trimmed Mirador de Daraxa (Daraxa lookout) was a lovely place for palace denizens to look onto the garden below.

Patio de los Leones

Courtyard in Granada

Price - adult/12-15yr/under 12yr €14/8/free

Hours - 8.30am-8pm Apr–mid-Oct, to 6pm mid-Oct–Mar, night visits 10-11.30pm Tue-Sat Apr–mid-Oct, 8-9.30pm Fri & Sat mid-Oct–Mar

Contact - http://alhambra-patronato.es; 958 02 79 71

Location - Granada, Spain

The celebrated Patio de los Leones (Lion Courtyard) sits at the core of the Palacio de los Leones, the palace built in the Alhambra in the second half of the 14th century by Mohammed V. Its best-known feature is its 11th century marble fountain with 12 spewing marble lions.

The patio's four water channels, running to and from the central fountain, represent the four rivers of Islamic paradise while the 12 lions could symbolise any number of things, perhaps the 12 signs of the zodiac, perhaps the 12 hours of the day. The courtyard's layout, which uses the proportions of the golden ratio, demonstrates the complexity of Islamic geometric design – the 124 slender columns that support the ornamented pavilions are placed in such a way that they are symmetrical on numerous axes.

San Sebastián

Framed by golden beaches and lush hillsides, San Sebastián has undeniable allure, from its venerable dining scene to its grand architecture and packed cultural calendar.

Culinary Superstar

San Sebastián has a justly deserved reputation as one of the world's great dining destinations. This is a city that celebrates the art of eating well in all its many forms – whether snacking on fresh oysters and txakoli (a lightly sparkling white wine) at a seaside cafe or lingering over a decadent, multi-course feast in a Michelin-starred dining room. Pintxos (Basque tapas) bars litter the streets of San Sebastián, and showcase first-rate ingredients from the surrounding coast and countryside combined with the culinary creativity of Basque chefs. When it comes to cooking, no other city quite compares.

Seaside Setting

Spain's culinary capital is also blessed with an alluring coastline. The long Playa de la Concha is the city's great backyard, a picturesque sweep of sandy beach that fronts gently lapping seas. Surfers head one beach over to the powerful waves that roll in off of Playa de la Zurriola, just behind the hipster enclave of Gros. Just offshore of the old town lies Isla de Santa Clara, a small hilly island that makes a fine getaway on a steamy afternoon. The city has some fine vantage points to gaze over its coastline, including the hilltop heights of Monte Urgull and Monte Igueldo.

Captivating Culture

For a city of its size, San Sebastian has a staggering array of festivals and cultural events. The International Film Festival, which happens in September, brings European and Hollywood stars to town, while the Semana Grande in August features a week of street parties and revelry. There's also music festivals, massive culinary fairs and folk fests that celebrate Basque culture in its myriad forms. Big events aside, there's always something happening in San Sebastián, with performances at the cutting-edge Kursaal, the belle époque Teatro Victoria Eugenia or the Tabakalera – the city's newest arts space.

A Grand Design

Once a favourite destination for Spanish royalty, San Sebastián has lost none of its lustre over the years. Elegant art nouveau buildings, ornate bridges and beautifully manicured parks and plazas create a captivating backdrop to this seaside city. Far from being mere set pieces, the grand architecture remains an integral part of San Sebastián, from the lavish Hotel Maria Cristina to the belle époque spa perched over the shoreline. Meanwhile, the old buildings lining the cobblestone streets of the Parte Vieja have been given new life with charming guesthouses, colourful boutiques and buzzing pintxos bars all part of the great and vibrant mix that is San Sebastián.

Experiences in San Sebastián

La Fábrica

Top choice basque restaurant in Parte Vieja

Price - mains €15-20, menús from €28

Hours - 12.30-4pm & 7.30-11.30pm Mon-Fri, 1-4pm & 8-11pm Sat-Sun

Contact - http://www.restaurantelafabrica.es; 943 98 05 81

Location - Calle del Puerto 17, San Sebastián, Spain

The red-brick interior walls and white tablecloths lend an air of class to this restaurant, whose modern takes on Basque classics have been making waves with San Sebastián locals over the last couple of years. At just €25, the multi-dish tasting menú is about the best-value deal in the city. Advance reservations are essential.

Aquarium

Top choice aquarium in Parte Vieja

Price - adult/child €13/6.50

Hours - 10am-9pm Jul & Aug, 10am-8pm Mon-Fri, 10am-9pm Sat & Sun Easter-Jun & Sep, shorter hours rest of year

Contact - http://www.aquariumss.com

Location - Plaza Carlos Blasco de Imaz 1, San Sebastián, Spain

Fear for your life as huge sharks bear down behind glass panes, or gaze in disbelief at tripped-out fluoro jellyfish. The highlights of a visit to the city's excellent aquarium are the cinema-screen-sized deep-ocean and coral-reef exhibits and the long tunnel, around which swim monsters of the deep. The aquarium also contains a maritime museum section. Allow at least 1½ hours for a visit.

San Telmo Museoa

Museum in Parte Vieja

Price - adult/student/child €6/3/free

Hours - 10am-8pm Tue-Sun

Contact - http://www.santelmomuseoa.com; 943 48 15 80

Location - Plaza Zuloaga 1, San Sebastián, Spain

Although it's one of the newest museums in the Basque Country, the San Telmo Museoa has actually been around since the 1920s. It was closed for many years, but after major renovation work it reopened in 2011. The displays range from historical artifacts to the squiggly lines of modern art, with all pieces reflecting Basque culture and society.

Labelling is in Spanish and Basque, but there are free audio guides available in other languages. If you don't speak Spanish, take one of these audio guides as otherwise the connections between the collection's pieces will seem vague.

Playa de la Concha

Top choice beach in New Town & Monte Igueldo

Fulfilling almost every idea of how a perfect city beach should be formed, Playa de la Concha (and its westerly extension, Playa de Ondarreta), is easily among the best city beaches in Europe. Throughout the long summer months a fiesta atmosphere prevails, with thousands of tanned and toned bodies spread across the sands. The swimming is almost always safe.

Parque de Cristina Enea

Top choice park in San Sebastián

Location - Paseo Duque de Manda, San Sebastián, Spain

Created by the Duke of Mandas in honour of his wife, the Parque de Cristina Enea is a favourite escape for locals. This formal park, the most attractive in the city, contains ornamental plants, ducks and peacocks, and open lawns.

Monte Igueldo

Viewpoint in New Town & Monte Igueldo

Hours - 10am-10pm Jun-Sep, shorter hours rest of year

Contact - http://www.monteigueldo.es

Location - San Sebastián, Spain

The views from the summit of Monte Igueldo, just west of town, will make you feel like a circling hawk staring down over the vast panorama of the Bahía de la Concha and the surrounding coastline and mountains. The best way to get there is via the old-world funicular railway to the Parque de Atracciones, a slightly tacky theme park at the top of the hill.

Individual rides (which include roller coasters, boat rides, carousels and pony rides) cost between €1 and €3. Trains on the funicular railway depart every 15 minutes.

Kursaal

Notable building in Gros

Contact - http://www.kursaal.eus; 943 00 30 00

Location - Zurriola Hiribidea 1, San Sebastián, Spain

Designed by Rafael Moneo, the Kursaal is one of the city's most beloved, and noteworthy buildings. Consisting of two cubes made of translucent glass, the structure, which serves as San Sebastián's cultural and conference centre, was designed to represent two beached rocks. A lively array of musical and cultural events are held here year-round.

The building is a useful landmark and has a great restaurant and bar. Drivers should note that there's a large public car park beneath, which provides handy access to Playa de Gros.

Hotel Maria Cristina

Historic building in New Town & Monte Igueldo

Contact - http://www.starwoodhotels.com; 943 43 76 00

Location - Paseo de la República Argentina 4, San Sebastián, Spain

A wonderful example of belle époque architecture, the Hotel Maria Cristina was designed by Charles Mewes, the architect responsible for the Ritz hotels in Paris and London. It first opened its doors in 1912; the first guest was the regent of Spain, Maria Cristina. Today, anyone can enter the lobby and admire the understated luxury, or browse the items on sale at the San Sebastián Food Gourmet Shop.

Iglesia de San Vicente

Church in Parte Vieja

Hours - 9am-1pm & 5-8pm Mon-Fri

Location - Calle de San Vicente 3, San Sebastián, Spain

Lording it over the Parte Vieja, this striking church is thought to be the oldest building in San Sebastián. Its origins date to the 12th century, but it was rebuilt in its current Gothic form in the early 1500s. The towering facade gives onto an echoing vaulted interior, featuring an elaborate gold altarpiece and a 19th-century French organ. Also impressive are the stained glass rose windows.

Navarran Pyrenees

Awash in greens and often concealed in mists, the rolling hills, ribboned cliffs, clammy forests and snow-plastered mountains that make up the Navarran Pyrenees are a playground for outdoor enthusiasts and pilgrims on the Camino de Santiago. Despite being firmly Basque in history, culture and outlook, there is something of a different feeling to the tiny towns and villages that hug these slopes. Perhaps it's their proximity to France, but in general they seem somehow more prim and proper than many of the lowland towns. This only adds to the charm of exploring what are, without doubt, some of the most delightful and least exploited mountains in western Europe.

Driving through this beautiful region is a pleasure. As you bear northeast out of Pamplona on the N135 and ascend into the Pyrenees, the yellows, browns and olive greens of lower Navarra begin to give way to more-luxuriant vegetation before the mountains thunder up to great Pyrenean heights, following the path of the Camino de Santiago.

Happy wanderers on wheels can drift around a network of quiet country roads in the area, stopping in pretty villages along the way. A couple of kilometres south of Burguete, the NA140 branches off east to Garralda. Push on to Arive, a charming hamlet, from where you could continue east to the Valle del Salazar, or go south along Río Irati. Another option is to take a loop northeast through the beautiful Selva de Irati forest, with its thousands of beech trees that turn the slopes a flaming orange every autumn and invite exploration on foot (from the parking area several well-marked trails lead off for anything from 2km to 8.2km return). Eventually this route will link you up with the Valle del Salazar at Ochagavía. If you stick to the NA140 between Arive and Ochagavía, Abaurregaina and Jaurrieta are particularly picturesque.

Experiences in Navarran Pyrenees

Monastery Complex

Monastery in Roncesvalles

Price - church free; guided tours adult/child €4.30/2.50

Hours - 10am-2pm & 3.30-7pm Apr-Oct, shorter hours Nov-Mar

Contact - http://www.roncesvalles.es; 948 79 04 80

The monastery complex contains a number of different buildings of interest, including the 13th-century Gothic-style Real Colegiata de Santa María and a cloister containing the tomb of King Sancho VII (El Fuerte) of Navarra. Reportedly 2.25m-tall, he fought against the Muslims in the Battle of Las Navas de Tolosa in 1212.

La Cueva de Zugarramurdi

Cave in Valle del Baztán

Price - adult/child €4/2

Hours - 10.30am-8pm Jul & Aug, shorter hours rest of year

Contact - http://www.turismozugarramurdi.com

According to the Inquisition, these caves (also known as Cuevas de Las Brujas, or Caves of the Witches) were once the scene of evil debauchery. True to form, inquisitors tortured and burned scores of alleged witches here.

Selva de Irati

Forest in Navarran Pyrenees

Price - car parking €5

Contact - http://www.selvadeirati.com

This beautiful virgin forest, popular for its beech trees and peaceful waterways and accessible via a system of well-marked trails, is one of the best-preserved forest parks in all of Europe.

Museo de las Brujas

Museum in Valle del Baztán

Price - adult/child €4.50/2

Hours - 11am-7.30pm mid-Jul–mid-Sep

Contact - http://www.turismozugarramurdi.com

Playing on the flying-broomstick theme of the Cueva de Zugarramurdi, this museum is a fascinating dip into the mysterious cauldron of witchcraft in the Pyrenees.

Real Colegiata de Santa María

Church in Roncesvalles

Hours - 9am-8.30pm

Contact - 948 79 04 80

The 13th-century Gothic Real Colegiata de Santa María, a good example of Navarran Gothic architecture, contains a much-revered, silver-covered statue of the Virgin beneath a modernist-looking canopy worthy of Frank Gehry.

Costa Brava

Stretching north from Barcelona to the Spanish–French border, the Costa Brava ('rugged coast') is undoubtedly the most beautiful of Spain's three main holiday coasts. Though there's plenty of tourism development, this wonderfully scenic region of Catalonia also unveils unspoiled coves, spectacular seascapes, wind-battered headlands, coast-hugging hiking paths, charming seaside towns with outstanding restaurants, and some of Spain's finest diving around the protected Illes Medes.

Delightful stone villages and the majestic Romanesque monastery of Sant Pere de Rodes nestle in the hilly backcountry, cloaked in the south in brilliant-green umbrella pine. Inland, wander northern Catalonia's biggest city, Girona, home to a moodily atmospheric, strikingly well-preserved medieval centre and one of the world's top restaurants. Neighbouring Figueres is famed for its bizarre Teatre-Museu Dalí, foremost of a series of sites associated with eccentric surrealist artist Salvador Dalí, who fell, like many others, for the wild natural beauty of seaside Cadaqués.

Experiences in Costa Brava

Teatre-Museu Dalí

Top choice museum in Figueres

Price - adult/child under 9yr €14/free

Hours - 9am-8pm Jul-Sep, 10.30am-6pm Oct-Jun, closed Mon Oct-May, also open 10pm-1am Aug

Contact - http://www.salvador-dali.org

Location - Plaça de Gala i Salvador Dalí 5, Figueres, Spain

The first name that pops into your head when you lay eyes on this red castle-like building, topped with giant eggs and stylised Oscar-like statues and studded with plaster-covered croissants, is Salvador Dalí. An entirely appropriate final resting place for the master of surrealism, it has assured his immortality. Exhibits range from enormous, impossible-to-miss installations – like Taxi Plujós (Rainy Taxi), an early Cadillac surmounted by statues – to the more discreet, including a tiny, mysterious room with a mirrored flamingo.

'Theatre-museum' is an apt label for this trip through the incredibly fertile imagination of one of the great showmen of the 20th century. Between 1961 and 1974, Dalí converted Figueres' former municipal theatre, destroyed by a fire in 1939 at the end of the civil war, into the Teatre-Museu Dalí. It's full of illusions, tricks and the utterly unexpected, and contains a substantial portion of Dalí's life's work, though you won't find his most famous pieces here (they're scattered around the world).

Even outside, the building aims to surprise, from its entrance watched over by medieval suits of armour balancing baguettes on their heads, to bizarre sculptures outside the entrance on Plaça de Gala i Salvador Dalí, to the pink walls along Pujada al Castell and Carrer Canigó. The Torre Galatea, added in 1983, is where Dalí spent his final years.

Opening the show is Taxi Plujós; put a coin in the slot and water washes all over the occupant of the car. The Sala de Peixateries (Fishmongers' Hall) holds a collection of Dalí oils, including the famous Autoretrat

Tou amb Tall de Bacon Fregit (Soft Self-Portrait with Fried Bacon) and Retrat de Picasso (Portrait of Picasso). Beneath the former stage of the theatre is the crypt with Dalí's plain tomb, located at what Dalí modestly described as the spiritual centre of Europe.

After you've seen the more notorious pieces, such as climbing the stairs in the famous Mae West Room, see if you can track down a turtle with a gold coin balanced on its back, peepholes into a green-lit room where a mirrored flamingo stands amid fake plants, and Dalí's heavenly reimagining of the Sistine Chapel in the Palau del Vent (Palace of the Wind Room).

Gala, Dalí's wife and lifelong muse, is seen throughout – from the Gala Nua Mirant el Mar Mediterrani (Gala Nude Looking at the Mediterranean Sea) on the 2nd level, which also appears to be a portrait of Abraham Lincoln from afar (best seen from outside the Mae West room), to the classic Leda Atòmica (Atomic Leda).

A separate entrance (same ticket and opening times) leads into Dalí Joies, a collection of 37 Dalí-designed jewels. He designed these on paper between 1941 and 1970, and the jewellery was made by specialists in New York. Each piece, ranging from the disconcerting Ull del Temps (Eye of Time) to the Elefant de l'Espai (Space Elephant) and the Cor Reial (Royal Heart), is unique.

Casa Museu Dalí

Top choice house in Cadaqués

Price - adult/child under 8yr €11/free

Hours - 9.30am-9pm mid-Jun–mid-Sep, 10.30am-6pm mid-Sep–Jan & mid-Feb–mid-June, closed mid-Jan–mid-Feb, closed Mon Nov–mid-Mar

Contact - http://www.salvador-dali.org; 972 25 10 15

Location - Port Lligat, Cadaqués, Spain

Overlooking a peaceful cove in Port Lligat, a tiny fishing settlement 1km northeast of Cadaqués, this magnificent seaside complex was the residence and sanctuary of Salvador Dalí, who lived here with his wife Gala from 1930 to 1982. The splendid whitewashed structure is a mishmash of cottages and sunny terraces, linked by narrow labyrinthine corridors and containing an assortment of offbeat furnishings. Access is by semi-guided eight-person tour; it's essential to book well ahead, by phone or online.

The cottage was originally a mere fisherman's hut, but was steadily altered and enlarged by the Dalís. Every corner reveals a new and wondrous folly or objet d'art: a bejewelled taxidermied polar bear, stuffed swans (something of an obsession for Dalí) perched on bookshelves, and the echoing, womb-like Oval Room. The artist's workshop, containing two unfinished original works, is especially interesting. Meanwhile, Dalí's bedroom still has a suspended mirror, positioned to ensure he was the first person to see the sunrise each morning. The dressing room, decorated by Gala, is covered in photos of the couple with high-profile acquaintances including Picasso, Coco Chanel and even Franco. Post-tour, you're free to explore the olive-tree-strewn grounds (dotted with giant white eggs) and pale-aqua pool (with its hot-pink lip-shaped bench) independently.

If the Teatre-Museu Dalí in Figueres is the mask that the showman presented to the world, this is an intimate glimpse of Dalí's actual face.

Empúries

Top choice archaeological site in L'Escala

Price - adult/child €5.50/free

Hours - 10am-8pm Jun-Sep, to 6pm Oct–mid-Nov & mid-Feb–May, to 5pm & closed Mon mid-Nov–mid-Feb

Contact - http://www.mac.cat; 972 77 02 08

Location - Carrer Puig i Cadafalch, L'Escala, Spain

The evocative seaside archaeological site of Empúries, 1.5km northwest of central L'Escala, immerses you in a strategic Greek, and later Roman, trading port. A lively audio guide commentary (included in the Price) unravels the history of the Greek town in the lower part of the site, before leading up to the Roman town, with its reconstructed 1st-century-

BC forum. The museum exhibits the top finds, including a marble statue of Asclepius, Greek god of medicine, dating to the 2nd century BC.

Traders from Phocaea set up shop here in the 6th century BC at what is now the charming village of Sant Martí d'Empúries, then an island. Soon afterwards they founded a mainland colony, Emporion (Market), which remained an important trading centre and conduit of Greek culture to the Iberians for centuries.

In 218 BC Roman legions clanked ashore to cut off Hannibal's supply lines in the Second Punic War. Around 195 BC they set up a military camp and by 100 BC had added a town. A century later the Roman town had merged with the Greek one. Emporiae, as the place was then known, was abandoned in the late 3rd century AD, after raids by Germanic tribes. Later, an early Christian basilica and a cemetery stood on the site of the Greek town, before the whole place disappeared under the sands for a millennium until its excavation in the 20th century. Barely a quarter of the site has been excavated so far.

Points of interest in the Greek ruins include the thick southern defensive walls, the site of the Asklepíeion (shrine to the god of medicine) with a copy of his statue, and the agora (town square), with remnants of the early Christian basilica (4th to 7th centuries AD) and the Greek stoa (market complex) beside it.

The larger Roman town includes palatial Domus 1, source of many of the finest mosaics (displayed April to October only, for conservation purposes), and the newly excavated Roman baths. Outside the walls are the remains of an oval amphitheatre, dating to the 1st century BC.

Castell de Púbol

Top choice castle in Palafrugell & Around

Price - adult/concession €8/6

Hours - 10am-7.15pm mid-Jun–mid-Sep, 10am-5.15pm Tue-Sun mid-Mar–mid-Jun & mid-Sep–Oct, 10am-4.15pm Tue-Sun Nov-early Jan

Contact - http://www.salvador-dali.org

Location - Plaça de Gala Dalí, Palafrugell & Around, Spain

If you're intrigued by artist Salvador Dalí, the Castell de Púbol is an essential piece of the puzzle. Between Girona and Palafrugell (22km northwest of the latter, south off the C66), this 14th-century castle was

Dalí's gift to his wife and muse Gala, who is buried here. The Gothic-Renaissance building, with creeper-covered walls, spiral stone staircases and a shady garden, was decorated to Gala's taste, though there are surrealist touches like a grimacing anglerfish fountain and a pouting-lips sofa.

The life of Gala Dalí is fascinating in its own right, due to her entanglement with several pivotal figures in the first half of the 20th century. Gala married French poet Paul Éluard in 1917, had a two-year affair with pioneer of Dadaism Max Ernst, and then met Dalí in 1929. With Dalí's approval she continued to take lovers, though their loyalty to each other remained fierce. Russian-born Gala was as admired for her elegance as much as she was feared for her imposing manners. Within the castle you'll find a collection of her high-fashion ballgowns, including a red-brick-print number designed by Dalí himself.

In 1969 Dalí finally found the ideal residence to turn into Gala's refuge. At the age of 76, Gala preferred to flit in and out of Dalí's decadent lifestyle. Dalí was only permitted to visit the castle with advance written permission, a restriction that held considerable erotic charge for the artist.

Today the Castell de Púbol forms the southernmost point of Catalonia's 'Salvador Dalí triangle'. The sombre castle is almost an antithesis to the flamboyance of Figueres' Teatre-Museu Dalí and Dalí's seaside home in Port Lligat near Cadaqués.

To get here, catch a bus to Cruilla de la Pera from Girona (€3, 40 minutes, 10 to 19 daily) or Palafrugell (€3.05, 25 minutes, seven to 13 daily), and alight at the stop on the C66 then walk 2km south to the castle. Alternatively, take a train from Girona to Flaça (€3.30, 15 minutes, at least 15 daily), then taxi the last 5km.

Catedral de Girona

Top choice cathedral in Girona

Price - adult/student incl Basilica de Sant Feliu €7/5

Hours - 10am-7.30pm Jul & Aug, to 6.30pm Apr-Jun, Sep & Oct, to 5.30pm Nov-Mar

Contact - http://www.catedraldegirona.org

Location - Plaça de la Catedral, Girona, Spain

Towering over a flight of 86 steps rising from Plaça de la Catedral, Girona's imposing cathedral is far more ancient than its billowing baroque facade suggests. Built over an old Roman forum, parts of its foundations date from the 5th century. Today, 14th-century Gothic styling – added over an 11th-century Romanesque church – dominates, though a beautiful, double-columned Romanesque cloister dates from the 12th century. With the world's second-widest Gothic nave, it's a formidable sight to explore, but audio guides are provided.

Highlights include the richly carved fantastical beasts and biblical scenes in the cloister's southern gallery, and a 14th-century silver altarpiece, studded with gemstones, portraying 16 scenes from the life of Christ. Also seek out the bishop's throne and the museum, which holds the masterly Romanesque Tapís de la creació (Tapestry of the Creation); dating from the 11th or 12th century, the tapestry shows God surrounded by the creation of Adam, Eve, the animals, the sky, light and darkness. There is also a Mozarabic illuminated Beatus manuscript, dating from 975. The facade and belltower weren't completed until the 18th century.

Illes Medes

Top choice dive site in L'Estartit & the Illes Medes

Contact - http://www.gencat.cat/parcs/illes_medes; 972 75 17 01

Location - L'Estartit & the Illes Medes, Spain

The allure of the Illes Medes, seven islets off L'Estartit beach, lies in their range of depths (down to 50m), kaleidoscopic marine life, and underwater cavities and tunnels. Since being gazetted as a reserva natural submarina in 1983, this archipelago has seen marine species thrive, making it Spain's most popular destination for snorkellers and divers. As of 2010, the islets form part of the protected 80-sq-km Parc Natural del Montgrí, les Illes Medes i el Baix Ter.

On and around rocks near the surface are colourful algae and sponges, as well as octopuses, crabs and various fish. Below 10m to 15m, cavities and caves harbour lobsters, scorpion fish and groupers. With luck, you'll spot some huge wrasse. If you get down to the sea floor, you may see thornback rays or marbled electric rays. Bottlenose dolphins make appearances too.

Conclusion

Thank you for purchasing this Spain travel guide book, I hope it was of use to you. If you are looking for more travel guides, please visit my Amazon Author page: http://www.amazon.com/author/toddwright.

Made in the USA
Columbia, SC
11 February 2020

87809846R00205